Investigations Manual

Investigations Manual

Binder Hamlyn
Chartered Accountants

London
Butterworths
1985

England	Butterworth & Co (Publishers) Ltd, 88 Kingsway, LONDON WC2B 6AB
Australia	Butterworths Pty Ltd, SYDNEY, MELBOURNE, BRISBANE, ADELAIDE, PERTH, CANBERRA and HOBART
Canada	Butterworth & Co (Canada) Ltd, TORONTO and VANCOUVER
New Zealand	Butterworths of New Zealand Ltd, WELLINGTON and AUCKLAND
Singapore	Butterworth & Co (Asia) (Pte) Ltd, SINGAPORE
South Africa	Butterworth Publishers (Pty) Ltd, DURBAN and PRETORIA
USA	Butterworth Legal Publishers, ST PAUL, Minnesota, SEATTLE, Washington, BOSTON, Massachusetts, AUSTIN, Texas and D & S Publishers, CLEARWATER, Florida

© Butterworths & Co (Publishers) Ltd 1985

All rights reserved. No part of this publication may be reproduced or transmitted in any form or by any means, including photocopying and recording, without the written permission of the copyright holder, application for which should be addressed to the publisher. Such written permission must also be obtained before any part of this publication is stored in a retrieval system of any nature.

This book is sold subject to the Standard Conditions of Sale of Net Books and may not be re-sold in the UK below the net price fixed by Butterworths for the book in our current catalogue.

British Library Cataloguing in Publication Data

Investigations manual.
   1. Accounting   2. Investigations
   I. Binder Hamlyn (*Firm*)
   657   HF5657
   ISBN 0 406 14258 0

Typeset by Phoenix Photosetting, Chatham, Kent
Printed in Great Britain by
Thomson Litho Ltd, East Kilbride, Scotland

Preface

Many accountants regard investigative work as representing one of the pinnacles of the professional accountant's work. After all, much of this work fits closely the picture of a professional accountant as a person of independent mind and judgment seeking to establish for a client what are the facts of a case, assessing those facts and then suggesting what courses of action may be available and appropriate. It is the essence of this sort of work that each engagement is different from every other and that the accountant must bring to it an entirely open mind.

It may, therefore, seem paradoxical to prepare a manual for investigations. Does this not seem to suggest that investigations can be reduced to a stereotype, or at least court the danger that they are so reduced?

There are two principal reasons for preparing this manual. Firstly, some investigation work is prepared within a framework of rules. Many engagements are intended to produce reports that will be used eventually either in Stock Exchange documents or to support opinions given in such documents. In such cases, the investigating accountant must understand the rules within which the work is to be conducted and the nature of the work which is required. This manual attempts to describe those rules where they exist, the work which would be expected and the types of report which are to be given. Secondly, the first stage of many investigations generally involves the collection of considerable amounts of information. As many investigations are subject to great time pressure, it is important that this stage of the work should be undertaken as quickly and efficiently as possible.

This manual describes for various types of investigation, the subject areas which might be suitable for coverage in the final report and the types of information which should be obtained initially.

In the final analysis, no manual, checklist or aide memoire can replace the unbiased judgment of the independent professional mind. This manual is not, therefore, to be regarded as the final exhaustive solution. The 'Approach to Investigations' suggests that each engagement should be approached on its own merits in the light of the client's requirements, and the guidance provided by this manual should be regarded as a basis for the engagement not an exhaustive specification.

Christopher Swinson
Binder Hamlyn
April 1985

Contents

Preface   v

Chapter 1   The approach to investigations   1

Chapter 2   Long form reports   13

Chapter 3   Profit forecasts   71

Chapter 4   Listing particulars and Stock Exchange circulars   137

Chapter 5   Bank presentations   203

Index   213

Chapter 1

The Approach to Investigations

INTRODUCTION	1.01
PREPARATION	1.09
The preliminary review	1.09
Obtaining written instructions	1.13
Planning	1.17
FIELDWORK	1.25
Getting the facts	1.25
Verification work	1.31
Specific profit and working capital forecast work	1.33
REPORTING	1.34
Interpretation and evaluation	1.34
Writing the report	1.37
DOCUMENTATION	1.43
DETAILED GUIDANCE	1.49

INTRODUCTION

1.01 The approach to an investigation is different from the approach to an audit. An investigation is not an audit in accordance with generally accepted auditing standards, although it may be carried out by accountants who have already audited the accounts of the business under investigation for the relevant years, or who are required to report on a 'true and fair' basis.

1.02 On the one hand an investigation is more comprehensive than an audit and yet, on the other hand, it may exclude many steps which would be considered necessary parts of an audit. For example, in the case of an investigation to provide detailed information for an intending purchaser there may recently have been an audit on which the client is prepared to rely, with a consequent reduction in the verification work expected of the investigating account, or the client may be willing to accept certain risks of error which an auditor would not be entitled to accept.

1.03 In the case of an investigation, the objectives and thus the work to be carried out are set uniquely by the client's instructions.

1.04 From the client's point of view, the value of an investigation lies in the introduction of an independent, dispassionate view of particular proposals or difficulties. Thus above all, the investigating accountant's approach must be entirely flexible and wholly without any preconception of the results.

1.05 Although speed is often of paramount importance the investigating accountant should never be diverted from examining matters which may be germane to the purpose of the investigation or fail to ensure the accuracy of facts which are to be reported. Real or assumed deadlines or time pressures may lead the investigating accountant to believe that there is not sufficient time to get the facts and that, in the circumstances it is acceptable to base decisions on intuitive business judgments. The investigating accountant should avoid such temptation and should warn the client against the dangers of reaching uninformed decisions.

1.06 In other cases, the client may not be able to give a precise specification of the information he requires either because he may not realise the full extent of the information which may be required or the extent to which an investigating accountant can be of service to him. In consequence, the investigating accountant should constantly bear in mind the need to offer guidance about the information which should be obtained for the purpose of the particular investigation, and about the scope of work he is equipped to carry out.

1.07 In practice, an investigation can usually be divided into a number of phases:
Preparation
(a) The preliminary review.
(b) Obtaining written instructions.
(c) Planning.

4   *The approach to investigations*

Fieldwork
(a)   Ascertaining the facts.
(b)   Verification.
(c)   Specific profit and working capital forecast work.
Reporting
(a)   Interpretation and evaluation.
(b)   Writing the report.

1.08   Of course, these phases will not always be distinct.

PREPARATION

The preliminary review

1.09   When an accountant is invited to carry out an investigation he should immediately attempt to evaluate the feasibility of the proposals which give rise to the need for the investigation. This may normally be done in a brief review taking no more than a few hours or days.

1.10   The preliminary review might disclose that the proposals are not feasible in relation to the business under investigation, with the result that a detailed investigation might be abandoned with consequent saving of cost to the client. Alternatively the preliminary review might indicate that the client's initial instructions are not appropriate and that their scope may need to be reduced, extended, or otherwise amended as appropriate to save wasted time, effort and money.

1.11   The nature of the preliminary review will depend on the type of investigation, but might cover the following items, among others:
(a)   the availability of information;
(b)   the apparent reliability of available information; and
(c)   the practicability of the proposed timetable.

1.12   The preliminary review may often take the form of a preliminary meeting between the client and the partner and manager responsible for the engagement. Such meetings are of the utmost importance since they determine the subsequent conduct of the investigation. It is therefore important that comprehensive file notes should be prepared of the people present and the matters discussed at all such and any subsequent meetings.

Obtaining written instructions

1.13   In the first instance it is probable that only oral instructions or at best brief general written instructions will have been received from the client. In discussion with the client, the investigating accountant should then establish more precisely the purpose of the investigation and the scope of the work required. As soon as this stage has been reached written confirmation of the instructions should be obtained.

1.14 The written instructions should be as explicit as possible to avoid subsequent misunderstandings and to avoid unnecessary work. They should be reviewed to ensure that, at first sight, they will lead to a report on which the client can reasonably reach a decision. If not, they should be discussed with the client again and clarified.

1.15 In many cases, a client may ask an investigating accountant to assist in drafting the detailed instructions and ideally they should include:
(a) the timetable for the investigation;
(b) the extent to which secrecy is required;
(c) the rationale behind the client's request for the investigation;
(d) the scope of the investigation specifying the areas of operations to be covered (eg sales, stocks, management, profits etc) and the periods to be covered;
(e) the names of auditors, other professional advisers, vendors, employees, etc from whom information may be required and the client's confirmation of the investigating accountant's authority to approach them;
(f) the reports required, eg long form report, prospectus report, profit forecast report etc;
(g) any audit work specifically required by the purchaser;
(h) the bases of any adjustments to the accounts of the company under investigation, eg to bring them into line with those of an intending purchaser.

1.16 In the absence of written instructions from the client, the investigating accountant should write to the client describing his understanding of the oral instructions which have been received and the client should be asked to confirm receipt of the letter.

Planning

1.17 Careful planning is vital in any investigation work. Using the client's written instructions as a starting point the investigating accountant should try to identify the information likely to be required, and plan the way in which it is to be obtained and presented to the client.

1.18 In this process, a number of steps may be helpful:
(a) Tabulate the financial statements of the subject company for the period to be covered by the investigation.
(b) Consider the economic and commercial environment in which the company is operating.
(c) Plan the degree of emphasis to be given to various aspects of the work.
(d) Initiate liaison with other specialists and overseas associates who may be involved in the investigation.
(e) Identify sources of information.

Tabulate financial statements

1.19 As a first step the investigating accountant should obtain copies of the detailed financial statements of the company (or companies) to be investigated for the period to be covered by the investigation together with the accounts for at least one previous year. Accounts of any subsidiaries should also be obtained. The balance sheets throughout the period and the detailed profit and loss accounts should then be tabulated grouping insignificant items so that attention is concentrated on the salient features. This procedure helps to develop an understanding of the business being investigated and provides a basis for the preparation of questions to be put to the company and its auditors.

Consider the environment

1.20 The performance of a company cannot be evaluated if the investigating accountant is ignorant of the economic and commercial environment in which the company operates. Information about this environment will be of most benefit if it can be obtained at an early stage in the investigation. Thus in planning an investigation, the accountant should review the available sources of information about the markets in which the subject company is trading and should arrange for the collection of all the information which may assist him in his work.

Plan emphasis

1.21 The client's written instructions together with a review of recent financial statements should enable the investigating accountant to plan the emphasis to be given to various parts of the work.

Initiate liaison with other specialists and overseas associates

1.22 If it appears likely that specialist assistance will be required the specialists concerned should be informed as early as possible to ensure that they will be available at the appropriate time. It is unreasonable to expect immediate attention at a moment's notice.

1.23 Where it appears that assistance will be required from overseas associates, they should be informed as soon as possible, even if detailed instructions and timetables cannot be given at this early stage. When the work required from each overseas associate has been defined, they should be provided with detailed instructions of the scope of their work, and the timetables they are to follow. Overseas associates may not be aware of the detailed UK regulations connected with the investigation, eg Stock Exchange requirements, the instructions must be precise and should be supported by appropriate reference material. It may be necessary for the investigating accountant to visit overseas associates personally to review the work which has been performed and ensure that all necessary steps have been taken in compliance with UK requirements.

Sources of information

1.24 The success of an investigation depends upon the timely availability of information, which can only be assured if the investigation accountant identifies at an early stage the sources of the information which will be needed and makes the necessary arrangements. If it is necessary to discuss the company's accounts or affairs with the individual directors, the auditors or the company's staff, appointments should be made as soon as possible. If the client or the company being investigated has to produce forecasts or information, this work should also be set in motion as soon as possible, and timetables for its completion should be agreed.

FIELDWORK

Getting the facts

1.25 The principal sources of information required by the investigating accountant will usually be the management of the company being investigated, followed by that company's auditors.

The subject company

1.26 If sufficient people within the subject company are aware of the purpose of the investigation, it should be possible for the company's staff to prepare much of the detailed information required. If secrecy is required the investigating accountant should agree with the client how secrecy is to be maintained while the necessary information is obtained.

1.27 It is helpful for the investigating accountant to establish good relationships with the subject company's staff and to have general discussions with the company's management and staff while detailed information is being collected. Among other matters, the topics to be discussed might include:
(a) the nature of the business, its products, marketing policies, personnel, fixed assets, and special characteristics;
(b) the accounting policies adopted in respect of depreciation, research expenditure, asset rentals receivable or payable, goodwill, long-term contracts, bad debt provisions, etc;
(c) the basis of valuation of stock and work-in-progress;
(d) the possible existence of transactions with related parties;
(e) the accounting policies adopted in relation to companies acquired or sold during the period under review;
(f) the nature of any prior year adjustments and extraordinary items;
(g) the directors' remuneration; and in particular whether the remuneration has been tantamount to a withdrawal of profits rather than simply a recompense for work done;
(h) any major transactions or events which have taken place since the last balance sheet date;
(i) the value of the company's freehold and leasehold property; and whether there have been any recent professional valuations.

1.28 Any opinions given in an investigation report are those of the investigating accountant and his alone. He must therefore do sufficient work to sustain the opinions which are given. It would not normally be sufficient to rely upon hearsay opinion (although in particular cases the client's instructions may indicate that this may be done) nor would it be sufficient

8   The approach to investigations

necessarily to rely upon work carried out by the subject company's auditors. However, the extent of the work to be carried out during a particular investigation depends entirely upon the nature of the instructions provided by the client and upon any statutory or other regulatory requirements appropriate to the reports which we are called upon to provide. The following chapters describe in more detail the content of the work which may be required in particular circumstances.

The subject company's auditors

1.29 It is often advantageous for the investigating accountant to meet the subject company's auditors at an early stage in the investigation. The method of procedure might be as follows:
(a) Arrange a general discussion with the partner and staff involved, referring in particular to any difficult or special points.
(b) Review the audit working papers for the period to be covered by the report, and tabulate the main components of balance sheet and profit and loss account figures, (if this has not already been done during the planning stage of the investigation).
(c) Obtain detailed analyses of principal items included in the subject company's accounts, if the subject company has not already made these available.
(d) Discuss irregular or unusual movements in the financial statements which have been disclosed by tabulations.
(e) Establish the scope of the audit work carried out during the period under review and evaluate the reliability of the audited accounts.
(f) Calculate the effect of any changes in accounting bases during the period.
(g) If the auditors are also the subject company's tax advisers, tabulate the company's tax computations for the period under review noting the stage of agreement reached with the Inland Revenue and discussing the tax position generally. Careful scrutiny of the tax computations and correspondence may provide an indication of adjustments which may be relevant for the purpose of the report.

Establish other sources of information

1.30 Useful information may also be gleaned from such external sources as Companies House, the financial press, trade and house publications, trade organisations, published accounts of competitors, the Department of Trade, the Department of Industry, the Land Registry, the Inland Revenue and statistical services. Some of these other sources of information become of fundamental importance in the case of a newly developing company which has only a short history and little experience upon which the investigating accountant can draw or in the case of a company in an industry with specialist practices. In such cases it may be necessary to conduct extensive investigations into the trading performance of prospective competitors, and to review surveys of the market by trade and other organisations, publications, and any other available technical data. A good example of such a company would be a North Sea oil exploration company. Obviously, the investigating accountant will not be competent to express an expert opinion on the geological and other surveys of the area of sea bed being explored by the company, but he will be in a position to collate all the available information and draw conclusions.

Verification work

1.31 The amount of any verification work to be performed by the investigating accountant will depend on the scope of the client's instructions and upon an assessment of the work done by the company's auditors. If it is felt that the audit work was inadequate the investigating accountant should consider to what extent additional work is required.

1.32 The review of the auditor's working papers can be difficult because the layout of audit working papers and the information contained therein differs from one firm to another. Although a perfectly adequate audit may have been carried out by the auditors it might not immediately appear so, simply because the audit files are not laid out in a form readily recognised by the investigating accountant. In assessing the work done the investigating accountant may attempt to decide independently what audit work he would have performed and compare this with what has been recorded as having been done and what the auditor says he has done. Alternatively, the investigating accountant may attempt to record the work that has been done on his own standard audit programmes to identify any apparent deficiencies.

Specific profit and working capital forecast work

1.33 Detailed work is also required to review the calculations of profit forecasts which may be a vital part of the information about the company being investigated. The work which might be undertaken in this connection is described in Chapter 3.

REPORTING

Interpretation and evaluation

1.34 By the time the investigating accountant has completed the phases of planning, gathering information, verification and forecast work, he will have learned a great deal about the business under investigation and will need to review, once again, the relevance of this information to the particular purpose of the investigation. He will be starting to form conclusions and will need to consider again what further information is required.

1.35 The skill of an investigating accountant lies in the ability to ask the right questions, to interpret and evaluate the information obtained, and from it to draw conclusions that will be meaningful to the client. To this end, he must consider not only the present situation, but also any factors that may be relevant to the client's intentions for the future. For example, if he is acting for an intending purchaser of a company or for an issuing house planning to sponsor a public issue of a company's shares, he should be looking

particularly for signs which might indicate flaws in the company's organisation or its future prospects. This may lead him to consider such questions as:
(a) The owner–manager may wish to be relieved of total responsibility for the company but proposes to stay on as manager with a service contract. Can he be relied on to invest as much effort in the company after he has sold his equity interest in the company?
(b) Do the company's existing products have a future?
(c) Is the company over dependent on a small number of major suppliers or customers? To what extent can these trading relationships be relied upon in the future?
(d) Is a key employee about to leave? Does the company offer the prospect of management continuity?
(e) Is the company subject to government or local authority regulations which may affect future profits (eg anti-pollution measures, etc)?

1.36 These are only a few of the questions that should be considered by the investigating accountant, and if full value is to be obtained from the information gathered in the course of the investigation, he must be alert to these and many other possibilities.

Writing the report

1.37 A preliminary outline of the form and content of the report should have been prepared at an early stage in the investigation and this will have been revised gradually as the investigation progressed. By the time the phases outlined above have been completed the form of the final report should have begun to crystallise. Indeed many sections should already be in rough draft form.

1.38 Investigation reports are usually merely an attempt to communicate any opinions which have been formed together with a great deal of information requested by the client or required to support the opinions which are being expressed. Great care should therefore be taken to ensure that the presentation of the report is of the highest quality. It should be concise and to the point. Jargon should be avoided and it should be intelligible to anyone likely to read it, eg bankers, legal advisers etc. Care should be taken to select the best way of presenting different pieces of information. In particular, the report must be unambiguous and great care must be taken to ensure that it is factually correct. To this end, a draft of the factual parts of the report should almost always be shown to those who have provided the information. It is too easy to misinterpret information given and thus perhaps to draw erroneous conclusions.

1.39 Where a number of people have been involved in drafting sections of the report, it is essential for one person to collate and edit these carefully to ensure that:
(a) different styles in writing are not apparent;
(b) the same terminology is used throughout;
(c) topics are not repeated; and
(d) one section does not conflict with another.

1.40 It is always worth remembering that a report takes much longer to write than one might think and as it is written a need for more information may become apparent. As much time as possible should be left for this stage of the investigation.

1.41 Before printing the report all those involved in the investigation should review it to ensure that:
(a) it provides the recipient with the information required;
(b) it is positive;
(c) it is factually correct;
(d) it is balanced—giving appropriate weighting to the good as well as the bad aspects of the business being investigated;
(e) it correctly reflects the investigating accountant's responsibility for the information reported and opinions expressed; and
(f) it conforms to any technical requirements.

1.42 In addition, it is often helpful, where time pressures permit, for the draft report to be read by a partner who was not involved in the investigation. A disinterested reader may be able to point out logical inconsistencies in the report or instances where evidence adduced does not support the opinion given.

DOCUMENTATION

1.43 The main objects of preparing investigation working papers are very similar to those of preparing audit working papers, namely;
(a) to provide a record of all the information obtained and the verification work carried out (if any) to enable the partner to form the opinion or make the recommendations to be contained in the report to the client;
(b) to enable the report to the client and the work upon which it is based to be independently reviewed and evaluated;
(c) to clarify the thinking of those by whom they are compiled; and
(d) to provide a sound basis upon which decisions can be made and thus justified in the event of subsequent challenge or enquiry.

1.44 It is almost axiomatic that investigations are conducted at great speed and require an ability to determine swiftly the direction and extent of the work. Far-reaching decisions may depend upon the accuracy and completeness of the information contained in any report. Consequently, it is important that a speedy and intelligent approach is combined with setting out the investigation working papers in a clear, concise and logical manner.

1.45 No standard format can be prescribed for all investigation files and working papers because of the varying objectives and types of investigation carried out. The amount and standard of documentation appropriate to support a report on a brief review will differ from that needed to support a report issued in connection with a prospectus.

1.46 However, whatever the type or object of the investigation the working paper files should contain:

12   *The approach to investigations*

(a) a copy of the client's instructions and timetable;
(b) a final draft of the report (all *important* figures should be cross-referenced to underlying schedules or should indicate the sources of information);
(c) copies of correspondence and minutes of meetings with client, auditors, company officials etc;
(d) working schedules detailing the work done and any conclusions drawn or recommendations made, including such items as:
   (1) detailed tabulations of accounts, schedules of adjustments;
   (2) comments on review of auditors working papers;
   (3) working papers supporting any specific verification or systems tests performed during investigation.

1.47 Other documents retained at the end of an investigation or schedules prepared should be filed in an order corresponding to the various sections of the report.

1.48 Often much of the information contained in an investigation report is not verified directly by the investigating accountant. When this is the case the report should indicate the source of such information, particularly if it is likely to be material to any final decision based on the report. Likewise, schedules and the documents reviewed during the investigation should *always* be annotated with the date of receipt and the name of the person who provided the information.

DETAILED GUIDANCE

1.49 The application of this general approach to particular types of investigation and the technical requirements applicable to them are discussed in the following chapters.

Chapter 2

Long Form Reports

INTRODUCTION 2.01

PRACTICAL GUIDES

    Investigation aides-memoire 2.1
      Section
        1 History
        2 Ownership
        3 General description of business
        4 Purchasing
        5 Manufacturing
        6 Selling
        7 Premises and plant
        8 Management and other employees
        9 Past financial results
       10 Trading results
       11 Balance sheets summary
       12 Stocks and work in progress
       13 Debtors and prepayments
       14 Bank and cash balances
       15 Creditors provisions and guarantees
       16 Taxation
       17 Debentures, long-term mortgages and loans
       18 Management accounting arrangements
Management and efficiency aides-memoire 2.2
Illustration of the contents of a long form report 2.3

INTRODUCTION

2.01 The reports which result from an investigation are as varied as are the tasks which an investigating accountant is called upon to perform. However, there are two basic types of reports which may be issued:
(1) Short form reports: ie reports which meet certain specific requirements often of a legal nature and which are often intended for publication (eg an accountant's report for a prospectus). Certain examples of such reports are described in later chapters.
(2) Long form reports: ie reports setting out the information which has been obtained by the investigating accountant and which are usually not intended for publication.

2.02 The information contained in a long form report may include both non-accounting and accounting information and depends entirely upon the needs of the investigating accountant's client.

2.03 Because the nature of investigations varies so widely, it is not possible to prescribe all the work which it will be necessary for the investigating accountant to perform and the information which should be given in any final report. General guidance can be given. Practical Guide **2.1** sets out a series of investigation aides-memoire which indicate the work which might be undertaken by an investigating accountant examining a company which a client proposes to acquire. The aides-memoire review each major aspect of the business and its accounts. Naturally in particular cases the aides-memoire will need amendment to reflect the nature of the business being investigated, the purpose of the investigation and the client's needs.

2.04 At each stage of the investigation, the investigating accountant should be assessing the quality of the information which has been gathered and the strengths of the business being investigated. In this context, the investigating accountant's experience is invaluable and cannot be replaced by a checklist. However, an aide-memoire can assist in the formation of judgments on an organisation and the management and efficiency aide-memoire (Practical Guide **2.2**) is intended for this purpose. It should be reviewed once the investigating accountant has completed gathering the basic information which is required.

2.05 Practical Guide **2.3** provides an example of the index and contents for a typical long form report. Each principal section in the example relates to a section of the investigation aides-memoire.

2.1 Investigation aides-memoire

The aides-memoire are intended to be used as guides to the procedures which should be undertaken in the course of a typical investigation.

It should be remembered however that each investigation is unique and must be tailored to the purpose for which it has been commissioned. Thus the aide-memoire is a foundation for an engagement not a detailed programme to be followed slavishly.

SECTION 1   HISTORY

1   Investigation objectives

To summarise the history of the company (group) and its ownership in so far as it is relevant to the engagement.

2   Source material to be obtained

(a) Charts showing the group structure.
(b) A summary of the changes in ownership of the company from its formation to the date of the engagement.
(c) Historical evidence of the formation of any group structure. Particularly note the vendors of shares, the consideration paid and any non-arm's length transactions.
(d) The memorandum and articles of association of the company.
(e) The company's minute books: copies of minutes of shareholders' and directors' meetings in recent years.

3   Procedures to be performed

(a) Carry out searches of all group companies' files at Companies House. Further specific searches should be performed in respect of connected parties, eg companies controlled by directors.
(b) Read directors' reports, chairman's statements and other official announcements made in the last five years.
(c) Read all minutes for directors' and shareholders' meetings in the last five years.

4   Discussion

Discuss this material with senior executives of the company.

5   Future arrangements

Discuss with management any proposed changes in the corporate or capital structure of the company.

SECTION 2 OWNERSHIP

1 Investigation objectives

To describe the present ownership of the company.

2 Source material to be obtained

(a) The rights attaching to the various classes of shares.
(b) The changes in capital during the period reviewed. Confirm that all shares issued other than for cash are on an arm's length basis.
(c) A summary of the present shareholders. Note any family relationships or family trust, directors' holdings, the ownership of nominee shareholders, if known, and the last transactions in the shares of the company. Group related shareholdings should be noted.
(d) Particulars of any share option scheme.
(e) Particulars of pre-emption provisions.

3 Procedures to be performed

(a) Compare the particulars shown by the search at the Registry of Companies with those stated in the Register of Members.
(b) Determine whether the company is a 'close company' for taxation purposes.

4 Discussion

Discuss the above material with the company secretary.

SECTION 3 GENERAL DESCRIPTION OF BUSINESS

1 Investigation objectives

To describe the general nature of the business and its development.

2 Source material to be obtained

(a) Historical evidence of the nature of the company's original business and any subsequent changes.
(b) Recent reports on the company or on any of its activities either produced internally or externally. Include any such reports becoming available during the investigation.
(c) Extel cards or brokers' circulars relating to the company or the industry.

3 Procedures to be performed

Read the company's board minutes, reports and public statements for the relevant period.

4 Discussion

Discuss this material with senior executives of the company.

5 Future arrangements

Discuss with management any new business ventures which are contemplated.

6 Management and efficiency aide-memoire

Review 'overall description' section.

SECTION 4 PURCHASING

1 Investigation objectives

To describe the nature of goods purchased by the company and the arrangements by which they are purchased.

2 Source material to be obtained

(a) Summaries of purchases for the last three years, subdivided by product, stating:
 (i) principal suppliers or sub-contractors;
 (ii) monetary value of purchases;
 (iii) details of processes undertaken by sub-contractors;
 (iv) discount rates and credit terms.
(b) Details of long term purchase contracts and significant outstanding purchase orders.
(c) Discount rates and credit terms.

3 Procedures to be performed

Relate this information to the company's trading accounts for the periods under review.

4 Discussion

Discuss the information with the chief buyer. Establish whether alternative sources of supply exist and whether alternative materials can be used.

5 Future arrangements

(a) Consider the company's long-term purchasing requirements and arrangements.
(b) Consider whether the company is dependent on particular suppliers.

6 Management and efficiency aide-memoire

Review the section on production management.

SECTION 5 MANUFACTURING

1 Investigation objectives

To describe the technical basis of the company's business.

2 Source material to be obtained

(a) Epitomes of all patents, licence agreements, trade marks, copyrights, and registered designs.
(b) Any articles written for non-specialist readers on the technical processes used by the company (or industry) including those published by the company, trade journals, the Trade Association and newspaper articles.
(c) The company's sales literature.

3 Procedures to be performed

(a) Relate the epitomes of patents etc to the details of licence payments paid and received, patent office fees paid, etc. Determine which have been financially important to the business.
(b) Where the patents etc constitute important present or future assets of the business, confirm that the company's legal title to the patent, etc is adequate.
(c) Establish the termination date of patents etc which have been financially important to the business.
(d) Obtain details of expenditure on research and development summarised by project.

4 Discussion

Visit the plant and discuss the company's production techniques with the technical executives of the business. Although an investigating accountant is not qualified to comment on technical aspects of production techniques and factory efficiency, as an intelligent observer it is possible to form an impression as to, eg whether facilities were cramped or under-utilised. Discuss the control of research and development expenditure and its achievements and expectations.

5 Management and efficiency aide-memoire

Review the section on production management.

6 Future arrangements

(a) Determine the effect on production arrangements of planned or likely changes in, or modification to, products manufactured, including alterations to the volume of production.
(b) Discuss the effect of planned or likely reorganisations to factory

facilities including the introduction of new machinery or processes and the elimination of inefficient machines or processes.
(c) Ascertain the importance of individual patents, etc to the future of the business. Consider the effect of the expiration of the patents.
(d) Discuss future research projects and their relationship to future marketing and production plans. Ascertain the cost, timetables and benefits involved.

SECTION 6 SELLING

1 Investigation objectives

To establish the company's sources of income.

2 Source material to be obtained

(a) Summaries of sales for the last three years by:
 (i) product type, in terms of volume and value;
 (ii) significant customers;
 (iii) sales branch or representative;
 (iv) geographical area, UK (by region) and overseas;
 (v) settlement terms—cash or deferred finance.
(b) The monthly totals of sales for the last two financial years and for all months of the current financial year.
(c) Details of the current sales order statistics available to management.
(d) Sales literature given to customers.
(e) Any long term sales contracts.
(f) Any warranties normally given to customers.
(g) Any recent market appraisals—the trend of the market shares taken by the company's products—its principal competitors—its product image.
(h) The trend of prices for products.

3 Procedures to be performed

Relate the above information to the company's trading accounts for the periods under review.

4 Discussion

Discuss this information with the marketing executive. Clarify the selling methods adopted and the method of determining selling prices. Consider the 'lead time' to convert sales orders into deliveries. Determine the distribution methods used.

5 Future arrangements

(a) Obtain particulars of any new products under development.
(b) Consider the sales revenue in the profit forecast in the light of the above information.
(c) Consider the effect of legislation affecting product pricing.

6 Management and efficiency aide-memoire

Complete the marketing section.

SECTION 7 PREMISES AND PLANT

1 Investigation objectives

To describe the fixed assets of the company.

2 Source material to be obtained

(a) Fixed assets totals
   (i) Summaries by asset headings at the end of each of the financial periods under review, together with totals of movements in the periods.
   (ii) Additions since the last audited financial statements, current capital commitments, and the capital expenditure budget for the next year.
(b) Premises—(stating separately particulars of freeholds, long leaseholds and short leaseholds)
   (i) Addresses, square footage by department, age, date of occupation, whether premises are available for development, planning consent position.
   (ii) Leases—tenure, annual rent, rent reviews, lessors, repair and other conditions of leases; similar particulars for sub-tenants.
   (iii) Cost, depreciation and written down value of individual premises at last financial reporting date.
   (iv) Profits and losses on sales of premises during periods under review.
   (v) The current valuation of premises—obtain copies of reports where relevant and establish the basis of valuation.
(c) Plant (including furniture, equipment, vehicles, tools)
   (i) Description, cost and dates of purchase for the principal items under these headings.
   (ii) Vehicles owned, their cost, drivers of private cars, and arrangements for charging mileage.

3 Procedures to be performed

(a) Physical aspects
   (i) Inspect significant items of premises and plant, and record your impression of them, including their state of repair.
   (ii) Examine asset register. Determine when assets were last physically verified—Discuss idle plant.
   (iii) Review insurance cover.
(b) Basis of capitalisation
   (i) Review basis of capitalisation of expenditure particularly treatment of overheads and design costs. Ascertain overall amounts of expenditure on items below minimum capitalisation figure. Note any non-arm's length transactions.
   (ii) Ascertain accounting treatment for capital grants.
(c) Basis of depreciation
   (i) Review depreciation rates, and methods—ensure that they appear to be relevant to the business. Restate where necessary.
   (ii) Determine that depreciation calculations have been consistently applied.

(iii) Where tooling has been capitalised ensure that life adopted does not exceed that of product manufactured.
(d) Basis of valuation
Ascertain whether this is on existing use basis, alternative use basis, or on the basis of depreciated replacement cost.

4 Discussion

These matters should be discussed with a senior executive responsible for capital investment.

5 Review of auditor's working papers

Establish that title verification by the auditors has been satisfactory that the auditors have adequately reviewed additions and that only items of lasting value have been capitalised.

6 Future arrangements

(a) Consider whether the premises are adequate for the development of the business. If appropriate review planning permissions.
(b) Determine whether the capital expenditure budget is reasonable in relation to the plans of the company.
(c) Ensure that future plans do not give rise to the redundancy of present facilities.
(d) Consider the future availability of capital grants.

7 Management and efficiency aide-memoire

Complete the 'property and plant' section.

SECTION 8   MANAGEMENT AND OTHER EMPLOYEES

1 Investigation objectives

To provide particulars of the company's management and staff relevant to an evaluation of operations of the company.

2 Source material to be obtained

(a) Directors
   (i) Names, qualifications, duties, ages, length of service, terms of service agreements, current salaries, commissions or bonuses, company pension contributions, cars provided and other fringe benefits.
   (ii) The analysis of directors' emoluments stated in the accounts for the periods under review.
   (iii) Shareholdings and family relationships.
(b) Senior management
   (i) Similar information to (a)(i) in respect of all senior management.
(c) Other employees
   (i) Numbers of staff analysed as appropriate eg between UK and other countries, by department, male and famale, weekly and four weekly paid, skilled and unskilled (production employees) etc, full-time, part-time or casual.
   (ii) Basis of payment by department, eg fixed weekly pay, time or piece work, commission basis, overtime premiums, etc.
   (iii) Average rates of pay.
(d) Pension schemes
   Groups of employees covered. Establish the cost to the company, the benefits provided, the actuarial position of the scheme, whether there are any unfunded past services contributions and the scheme's relationship to legislation. Does the company have any moral obligations towards persons not in the scheme.
(e) The pension scheme and other information booklets given to new employees.

3 Procedures to be performed

Relate the above information to the organisation chart, trading accounts and management accounting returns for the periods under review.

4 Discussion

(a) Discuss the employee particulars with the company's personnel manager. Note the trend of labour costs, the effect of union activities and government legislation on rates of pay. Ascertain the date and rate of the last wage claim. Consider the future availability of labour and the possibility of automation. Assess the adequacy of pension and staff welfare arrangements. Consider compliance with contract of employment regulations.
(b) Consider whether there is any evidence that the payment of personal tax

has been avoided eg by charging private items against company profits or omitting to deduct PAYE from employees' emoluments.

5 Future arrangements

Assess the future continuity of management.

6 Management and efficiency aide-memoire

Complete the personnel management section.

SECTION 9   PAST FINANCIAL RESULTS

1   Investigation objectives

To summarise the past financial results of the company in relation to the continuing business.

2   Source material to be obtained

(a)   Copies of the audited accounts for all the years under review (usually five together with the year preceding the first year), ensuring the auditors' and directors' reports, and the chairman's statements are produced.
(b)   Copies of the detailed management trading and profit and loss accounts including costing variance statements, for the period under review.
(c)   Summaries of all balance sheet figures at all the accounting dates.
(d)   Analyses of unusual profit and loss figures for the periods under review.

3   Procedures to be performed

(a)   Tabulate this information.
(b)   Calculate significant ratios and percentages.

4   Discussion with management

Discuss this information with the company's management. Obtain explanations for meaningful and significant variations. Identify the significant accounting policies in relation to the accounts and the consistency of their application in the periods under review.

5   Review of auditors' working papers

Whatever summarised comments are made in the report eventually submitted to the client, a memorandum should be included in the investigation working papers fully explaining the conclusion reached on the review of auditors.
By discussion, and the examination of working papers, determine whether:
(a)   the audit was performed by persons with adequate technical training and proficiency;
(b)   due professional care was exercised;
(c)   the work was adequately planned and properly supervised;
(d)   an adequate review was made of internal control arrangements and whether the auditors' checks on systems confirmed the operation of the controls—determine the extent of such checks—obtain copies of letter of recommendation;
(e)   the auditors' working papers record the steps taken by them to form an opinion on the accounts;
(f)   additional services provided by the auditors to the company gave rise to doubts about their independence.

Discuss with the auditors any qualifications in their reports. Ascertain the extent of the qualifications. Consider whether, with the benefit of hindsight, qualifications are still relevant.

6 Further work to be undertaken

The need to undertake additional work of an audit nature may arise:
(a) if required by the specific terms of reference of the investigation;
(b) if the investigating accountant is not satisfied that the work performed by the auditors and the information produced is sufficient to explain adequately the past financial results of the entity and to confirm that the final balance sheet gives a true and fair view;
(c) if it is necessary to avoid a technical qualification in a formal report for Stock Exchange purposes.

7 Management and efficiency aide-memoire

Review the financial management section.

SECTION 10   TRADING RESULTS

1 Tabulating results

The format to be used will depend on the business performed and the management accounting arrangements. The following format could be adopted, with the individual years presented side by side and separate schedules supporting individual elements.

	£	%
Sales		100
Cost of sales		
Gross margin	____	____
Overheads		
Administration		
Selling		
Finance		
Directors' remuneration	____	____
	____	____
Profit before exceptional items and taxation		
Exceptional items	____	____
Profit before taxation		
Taxation	____	____
Profit after taxation		
Extraordinary items		
Dividends	____	____
Profit retained		
Distributable profits brought forward		
Distributable profits carried forward	====	====
Earnings per share	____	____
Dividend %	____	____
Dividend cover	____	____

30 *Investigation aides-memoire*

2 Discussion

Discuss the profit and loss accounts with the chief accountant and other senior managers.

(a) These statements are of major importance in the accountants' report and usually more time should be devoted to them than to, eg property and plant.
(b) The revenue attributable to principal elements of the business should be identified and gross profit percentages explained. If the accounting arrangements do not readily provide this information attempts should be made to reconstruct it.
(c) Many businesses suffer a 'shrinkage' in the gross margins which may theoretically be expected. A manufacturing concern may suffer production inefficiencies, excess labour and material costs etc. If the accounting system does not measure such losses their effect should be estimated.
(d) Overhead expenses should be analysed by function, eg factory, administration and selling; by department eg quality control, purchasing etc; and by expense category eg salaries, rent and rates etc. Significant expense variations should be identified and explained.
(e) Establish where these profits have been 'window dressed' eg by the reduction of cash expenditure on research, advertising or maintenance in particular periods.
(f) Transactions with directors or related companies should be identified and, if not on an arm's length basis, they should be explained.
(g) Ensure that all reserve movements during the period under review are traced and explained.
(h) Compare the profit and loss account for the last year under review with the original budgeted figures for the year.

3 Matters to be discussed with auditors

Establish whether:

(a) the accounts including the consolidated accounts, were prepared on appropriate accounting policies consistent with those applied in previous periods;
(b) the audit working papers contained schedules showing the composition of significant individual items in the statutory profit and loss accounts;
(c) satisfactory explanations were received for all significant variations in income and expenditure:
 (i) compared with previous years;
 (ii) compared with budget;
(d) there were any credits or debits relating to prior years' revenue or costs which were not disclosed;
(e) all significant exceptional and extraordinary items were disclosed;
(f) all significant changes in basis of accounting were disclosed;
(g) the directors of the holding company (or past directors or their dependants) received any emoluments or other benefits either in cash or kind;
(h) the auditors had any knowledge of any transactions that have taken place between the companies (or group companies) and directors.

SECTION 11 BALANCE SHEETS SUMMARY

1 Tabulating balance sheets

The format considerations are the same as those which apply to the profit and loss accounts. The format could be:

FIXED ASSETS		
Tangible fixed assets		x
Intangible fixed assets		x
		x
CURRENT ASSETS	x	
Less: Current liabilities (due with one year)	(x)	
		(x)
		x
Creditors (due in more than one year)		(x)
		x
Provisions and long-term liabilities		(x)
		x
SHARE CAPITAL		x
RESERVES		x
		x

2 Discussion

Discuss the balance sheets with the chief accountant.
(a) The scrutiny of the summarised details of each of the balance sheet figures should highlight significant variations, changes in accounting principles, etc.
(b) All amounts due to/from related parties (directors and associate companies etc) should be identified.
(c) As far as possible ascertain the present value of all balance sheet items.
(d) If the business produces CCA or CPP restatements of the historical cost accounts, determine the nature of the significant adjustments between the two sets of figures.

3 Review of auditors' working papers

Establish that the auditors have made a critical review of the items in the balance sheets (especially the last balance sheet) with particular reference to:

(a) the basis on which the amounts are stated;
(b) the existence, ownership and proper custody of assets;
(c) the existence of liabilities;
(d) the relationship between the corresponding figures;
(e) the suitability of the descriptions used; and
(f) adequate disclosure of information.

SECTION 12   STOCKS AND WORK IN PROGRESS

1   Source material to be obtained

(a) The summarised composition of stock figures at each of the accounting dates during the period under review.
(b) The basis of valuation for each significant stock category.
(c) Original stock sheets at each of the relevant accounting dates during the relevant period.

2   Tabulate the inventory details

(a) The tabulations should analyse stocks by location or product type, the material, labour and overhead cost elements of stocks and the provisions set up against stock value.
(b) Relate this information to the tabulated particulars or financial accounts for the periods under review.
(c) Determine the ratios of stocks to cost of sales, and to net profits.

3   Discussion

(a) Visit the premises and discuss this information with the company's production controller and chief accountant.
(b) In order to assess the quality of the company's reporting arrangements, discuss:
(i) operational controls—the various types of stock control records and reports—the differences revealed by such records;
(ii) physical aspects—the effectiveness of the annual or continuous stocktake procedures—the book/physical differences revealed by the stocktakes;
(iii) cut off—the arrangements made;
(iv) valuation—the treatment of material, labour and overheads—what overheads are included and the treatment of capacity variations—the review of variances;
(v) contract reviews—assessment of future losses and the method of taking profits;
(vi) clerical accuracy—the controls incoporated in the evaluation arrangements;
(vii) obsolescence—the assessment of provisions;
(viii) realisable value—the comparisons made between cost and future sales proceeds.

4   Review of auditors' working papers

(a) Examine the records of the auditors' attendance at the physical stocktakings or examination of continuous stocktaking.
(b) Study the record of work done by the auditors in relation to the matters listed in 3(b) above.
(c) Consider the results shown by the review of profit and loss gross margins.

34 Investigation aides-memoire

(d) Assess the consistency of the application of accounting principles and methods.
(e) Ascertain whether stocks have been deliberately manipulated eg to minimise taxation liabilities.

SECTION 13 DEBTORS AND PREPAYMENTS

1 Source material to be obtained

(a) Summarised particulars of trade and other debtors' figures and bad debt provisions during the period under review.
(b) The aged list of trade debtors at the last accounting date and at the current date.

2 Procedures to be performed

(a) Relate the above information to the tabulated particulars of financial accounts.
(b) Determine the overall ratios of debtors to sales and the actual number of month sales represented by debtors.
(c) Ensure that the debtor particulars are not at variance with the sales and marketing information.
(d) Agree the lists of debtors to the summaries.

3 Discussion

(a) Discuss debt collection performance with the credit controller. Review credit control arrangements and consider the company's bad debt experience. Consider whether, with hindsight, current evidence justifies the bad debt provision in the last accounts.
(b) Ascertain the accounting policy in relation to profit taking on sales contracts. Confirm the treatment of consignment sales, sales on deferred terms, and long-term sales contracts.

4 Review of auditors' working papers

(a) Review the results of the circularisation of debtors by the auditors.
(b) Determine the basis of the bad debt provision and review the work done by the auditors.
(c) Ensure that a proper review was made of after date credit notes.

5 Other debtors and prepayments

(a) Ensure that other debtors' figures do not reveal unusual variations.
(b) Enquire into the composition of significant elements.
(c) Identify any balances with directors, executives or companies controlled by directors or executives, or other related companies. The cause of such balances should be examined.

SECTION 14 BANK AND CASH BALANCES

1 Source material to be obtained

(a) Summarised particulars of cash/overdraft figures during the period under review.
(b) The bank reconciliations at the last year end.
(c) The cash particulars at the current date.

2 Procedures to be performed

Review the reconciliations and ensure that no anomalies arise.

3 Discussion

Discuss this information with the chief accountant and obtain details of unused facilities and the repayment terms and security given for bank overdrafts. Ensure the continuation of such arrangements. Establish whether the funds are in unremittable accounts overseas. Ascertain the borrowing powers of the company and ensure that the company has complied with any limits or other restrictions.

4 Review of auditors' working papers

Confirm that the balances shown in the most recent audited accounts were independently confirmed with the banks. Review the audit work on reconciliations and cash counts.

5 Adequacy of facilities

Consider:
(a) The cash position shown by the cash flow forecast or if no forecast has been prepared evaluate by other available indication of future cash flows.
(b) The alterations possible to the cash flow forecast due to:
(i) capital and research expenditure—the limitation of non-vital expenditure or the impact of further desirable expenditure;
(ii) inventories, debtors and creditors—the minimisation of funds employed and the maximisation of the use of resources;
(iii) profit retentions—the increase in sales and margins and the reduction of overheads;
(iv) variations in borrowing;
(v) the availability of further capital.

SECTION 15 CREDITORS PROVISIONS AND GUARANTEES

1 Source material to be obtained

(a) Summarised particulars of trade and other creditors for the period under review
(b) The list of trade creditors at the last accounting date.
(c) The control accounts totals of creditors at the time of the investigation.
(d) Particulars of current capital commitments and outstanding orders from suppliers.

2 Procedures to be performed

(a) Relate this information to the particulars obtained concerning purchases and suppliers.
(b) Ascertain the period of credit taken from suppliers.
(c) Post balance sheet review:
 (i) scrutinise the cash book/purchase day book following the last accounting date;
 (ii) examine current year management reports/profit forecasts/budgets for details of omitted liabilities.

3 Discussion

Discuss this information with the chief accountant. Ascertain the accounting policies adopted in relation to significant provisions and guarantees such as warranties, and unfunded pension liabilities etc. Confirm that accruals are adequate.

4 Review of auditors' working papers

(a) Determine the extent to which liabilities and outstanding litigation have been verified by external confirmations.
(b) Review the evidence of verification of provisions.

5 Other creditors and accruals

Establish whether the figures for other creditors reveal unusual variations. Inquire into the composition of significant elements, identify any balances with directors, executives or companies controlled by directors or executives or other related companies. The source of such balances should be examined. Inquire into the calculation of such items as royalties and warranties.

6 Commitments

(a) Ensure that outstanding orders on suppliers are not at onerous prices.
(b) Confirm that adequate funding arrangements exist for capital commitments.

7 Contingent liabilities

Review identified contingent liabilities under bills discounted, guarantees, litigation etc. Confirm that no actual liability has arisen.

SECTION 16 TAXATION

1 Investigation objectives

To state the taxation factors relating to the business.

2 Source material to be obtained

Normally the minimum documentation required would be as follows:
(a) copies of the most recent agreed computations;
(b) copies of the correspondence with the Revenue agreeing the computations;
(c) copies of the most recent 'shortfall' clearances;
(d) copies of subsequent draft computations;
(e) the composition of the tax account in the most recent balance sheet;
(f) the most recent deferred taxation computations.

3 Taxation specialist review

A review should be carried out by a taxation specialist and should deal with the following points at least:
(a) the liabilities and deferred taxation amounts in the most recent balance sheet, including the appropriateness of the provision for deferred taxation;
(b) details of the main adjustments to profits for taxation purposes;
(c) the tax effects arising from adjustments to profits made by us as part of our report;
(d) the reasons for any abnormal provisions;
(e) the years that have not been agreed with the Revenue;
(f) what matters are in dispute with the Revenue;
(g) if there is anything which needs to be disclosed to the Revenue;
(h) if the company is a 'close company' and, if so, any problems in relation to 'shortfall' assessments;
(i) extent of any unabsorbed tax losses and unrelieved advance corporation tax;
(j) details of the written down values of fixed assets for tax purposes compared with book figures;
(k) potential or actual capital gains tax liabilities;
(l) any factors, which a new owner should consider in relation to tax position of the company;
(m) whether the proposed transactions are being conducted in the best way for tax purposes and, if not, suggestions for improving the situation;
(n) whether any warranties should be obtained.

4 Period to be reviewed

The Revenue's right in the absence of fraud to reopen tax computations is limited to six years. Ideally the investigating accountant should review computations for the last six years. In practice, in the absence of unusual circumstances, the review may be limited to the last agreed computations plus the subsequent computations.

SECTION 17   DEBENTURES, LONG-TERM MORTGAGES AND LOANS

1 Source material to be obtained

(a) Summarised particulars of long-term borrowings for the relevant period.
(b) The agreements under which long-term borrowings have been provided.

2 Procedures to be performed

(a) Examine trust deeds, loan repayment terms, borrowing restrictions and other conditions.
(b) Review accounts during the period under review to ensure that the company has complied with all borrowing conditions.
(c) When reviewing cash facilities consider the maturity dates of obligations.

SECTION 18 MANAGEMENT ACCOUNTING ARRANGEMENTS

1 Investigation objectives

To identify the management reporting arrangements and to highlight their limitations.

2 Source material to be obtained

(a) Daily particulars of sales, production, cash, etc as submitted to management.
(b) Any similar weekly or monthly statistics.
(c) The sales and purchase order book position reports: the inventory reports.
(d) The monthly financial report, including cost reports and comparisons with budgets.
(e) The complete management accounting returns submitted to the board.
(f) Annual profit statements and budget comparison.
(g) The profit forecasts and budgets, including the cash forecast. Determine the period covered by such projections.

3 Procedures to be performed

(a) Relate the above information to the tabulated particulars of trading accounts for at least the most recent completed period. Ensure that the current year's reports are fully understood, particularly the most recent reports.
(b) Review the company's internal control systems, initially by letters of recommendation. If the review is inconclusive, perform limited follow-through tests on a small number of transactions.

4 Discussion

Discuss this information with the chief accountant. Determine the speed of reporting, who reviews the reports, the relevance and accuracy of the reports and the action resulting from reports.

5 Computer arrangements

Obtain details of computer applications. If these are extensive arrange for an appropriate computer specialist to review the company's computer policy and organisation.

6 Future arrangements

Consider whether the management accounting arrangements will facilitate proper management control in the future.

2.2 Management and efficiency aide-memoire

In conducting an investigation, an accountant is not simply attempting to identify facts or analyse information but more importantly to develop a critical understanding of the nature of the business under investigation, its organisation and aspects. In many cases, it is the development of this understanding through the application of experience that is of particular value to the client.

No checklist or aide-memoire can replace the judgment of the experienced accountant, but it is possible to indicate the areas of a business which should be considered in assessing the business. The management and efficiency aide-memoire is designed to fulfil this purpose. It is envisaged that once the investigation aide-memoire (see 2.01) has been used as a guide to the collection of information, the management and efficiency aide-memoire should be used as an aide to the formation of judgments on the organisation.

It should be remembered that each business is unique as is each investigation, and the aide-memoire may therefore include items which are not relevant in some cases and exclude items which are relevant in other cases.

OVERALL INTRODUCTION

Introduction

Before thinking about sales or production, for example, it is essential to get a clear picture of the state of the company as a whole. The framework within which specific functions are carried out has a strong influence on the eventual outcome, successful or otherwise of these functions. More important, it indicates whether the company is likely to go forward and develop or whether it will stagnate (or worse).

Some of the areas covered in this section in a general way—in order to get a quick overview of the company—are dealt with in more detail in later sections. The questions in this section are intended to enable you to gain a broad but clear picture of the state of the company as a whole by making sure you are informed about the company's:
(a) Aims;
(b) Policies;
(c) Profit motivation;
(d) Organisation;
(e) Leadership and morale;
(f) Strategic planning;
(g) Information systems.

Aims

The following questions are aimed at assessing the fundamental question 'where is the company going?'.

(a) Is it fairly clear what the directors want the company to achieve (eg increased turnover, profits, growth, rate of return, or customer satisfaction, bigger and better products, and so on)?
(b) Do people other than directors have the same, or similar, aims for the company?
(c) Have these aims been publicised within, or outside the company?
(d) Have they been quantified and formalised in a definitive statement?
(e) Are the aims reviewed from time to time?
(f) In very general terms, is it clear what business the company is in?

Policies

Most organisations operate within the framework of a set of basic policies, although often people in these organisations are unaware that such a framework exists. The company's policies are a set of principles or guidelines, on the basis of which functions and activities are carried out and decisions relating to these functions are made.

The following are a few questions aimed at finding out whether company policies encourage and stimulate development of the company or whether they tend to hinder it.
(a) Does the company policy on major issues seem to be fairly clear to:
 (i) the directors?
 (ii) other people in the company?
 (iii) third parties such as customers, suppliers, bankers, trade unions, etc?
 (iv) you?
(b) Has company policy on these issues been:
 (i) publicised in any way?
 (ii) published in a definitive statement?
(c) Is policy reviewed from time to time?

Profit motivation

The aims of the company usually include making a profit, expressed directly as such, or indirectly in terms of return on capital employed, dividend payout or growth, etc. People working for the company have their own personal aims (eg a higher salary, a better office). If the company is to be successful in the long term it is essential that the personnel, especially at supervisory levels and above, are in broad agreement with the company's aims. In particular this means that it is highly desirable that they should have strong positive feelings and reactions towards making profits. The following questions should help you to assess the strength of these feelings and reactions.
(a) Do personnel seem to take an interest in the published accounts (if any)?
(b) Have they expressed a wish for more information than is shown in these accounts?
(c) Where accounts are not published have personnel expressed a wish to have financial information about the company?
(d) Is it your impression that executives are 'figure conscious'. In particular do they take into account the likely effect on profits (or costs) of their decisions?

(e) Is it a feature of the way the company is run that personnel want or are expected to work to some cost or profitability yardsticks, no matter how unsophisticated these may be.

Organisation

Having gained an impression of where you think the company is heading, the policies it is pursuing, and the general attitude towards making profits, the following questions should help you to assess whether the company is sufficiently well organised to further its aims.
(a) Are executives clear about:
    (i) their duties and responsibilities?
    (ii) the extent of (or limit to) their authority?
    (iii) their organisational relationships with fellow executives (eg line and staff relationships)?
(b) Are these matters set out clearly in job descriptions?
(c) As a general rule do executives seem to conform to the organisational patterns laid down, rather than follow an informal 'underground' organisation?
(d) Do executives and personnel generally seem to know to whom they are responsible?
(e) Are people normally responsible to only one superior?
(f) Does it seem to you that the:
    (i) duties; or
    (ii) spans of responsibility
    are too much for some executives?
(g) Does there seem to be reasonable unity over important issues amongst the:
    (i) directors?
    (ii) senior or top executives?
    In fact can you say that there is a 'top management' which on the whole functions properly?
(h) Are the directors and senior executives mainly carrying out activities appropriate to their level within the organisation rather than being too involved in day-to-day operations and detail?
(i) Is reasonable use made of expert, functional specialists in the organisation?
(j) Are the major functions such as marketing, production, finance, personnel and, where appropriate, research and development and computer operations properly represented:
    (i) at all levels within the organisation?
    (ii) with appropriate status accorded, especially at the higher levels?
    (iii) with men of the right calibre?

Leadership and morale

Management—from supervisors to directors—must be able to influence and co-ordinate people and events, at least within their own areas of responsibility, if they are to achieve their objectives and carry out their responsibilities efficiently. (In this context 'people' refers to all those within the company, rather than to eg customers and suppliers.) Furthermore, this influence, or leadership, must be exercised without lowering or destroying morale—the general 'atmosphere', self-discipline and control in the company—that is, without 'upsetting the boat'.

It is very difficult, if not impossible, to establish objective criteria for the state of leadership and morale in a company. The following questions are intended to result in a few clues from which to form your own opinion.

(a) Are there adequate channels of communication within the organisation of the company enabling objectives, intentions, directives, policies, and the like—and objections to them—to be circulated between personnel at different levels of the organisation?
(b) Within reasonable limits do people especially executives in the company:
 (i) know each other?
 (ii) have contact with each other?
(c) Are the attitudes of people throughout the company satisfactory as regards their willingness to:
 (i) work well?
 (ii) accept responsibility?
(d) Is their general attitude positive. For example, are they keen to suggest improvements within the company rather than grumble and gossip?
(e) Generally speaking is the industrial relations records of the company over the past five years satisfactory?
(f) Generally does there seem to be:
 (i) reasonable loyalty to the company and its senior management?
 (ii) an absence of serious discontent and frustration?
 (iii) an attempt to relate the individual interest of each person in the company to those of the company itself (eg promotion with company growth)?

Strategic planning

Senior executives have to make decisions which can have radical effects on the nature and health of the business in several years time, or more. These decisions can even place the long term existence of the company at risk and once made are often irrevocable.

This situation results from a rapid increase, in recent years, in the:
(a) complexity and size of businesses;
(b) lead time between making decisions and feeling their effects;
(c) rate of technological change;
(d) types and intensity of competition;
(e) complexity of political, legal, economic, and social environment in which companies operate.

In this situation 'off-the-cuff' management may not be appropriate. Instead there is an increasing need for some form of strategic planning in order to ensure the company's survival and development.

Strategic planning as a subject is very extensive—here are a few of the more important questions you should consider.

(a) Can you recognise any form of strategic planning (covering a period beyond that of the normal operating budget) being carried out within the company?

(b) If yes, is this planning being carried out by the directors and senior executives?
(c) If directors and senior executives are planning strategically, are they doing so, as far as you can see, as a result of a conscious decision to be committed and identified with planning as opposed to ad hoc decision making?
(d) Do directors and executives appear to have a satisfactory understanding of:
   (i) any strategic plans which may have been formulated?
   (ii) the process by which plans have been prepared?
   (iii) the role everyone in the organisation must play in order to fulfil the plans?
(e) Are plans used as a basis for making immediate or short-term decisions ie are they translated into action programmes?
(f) Are formal procedures laid down as to the:
   (i) contents of plans?
   (ii) preparation of plans?
   (iii) review and appraisal of plans?
   (iv) monitoring of plans?
   (v) personnel who should take part in planning?
(g) Does the overall plan for the company include all major functions and activities ie is it comprehensive?
(h) Are the plans for separate functions and activities co-ordinated with each other?
(i) Do you think that strategic planning in the company is sufficiently complex or time consuming to warrant employing a planning specialist. If yes, does the company employ such a person?
(j) Generally speaking, if formal planning procedures exist in the company, do you think that the directors and senior executives see them as being of vital importance to the business. If yes, are the procedures given the status and priority corresponding to this importance?
(k) In your opinion is there anything which is likely to limit, or prevent, the company from implementing its plans?

Information systems

Over and above the communication of aims, policies etc, to which reference has already been made, information satisfies the continual need of the management of a company for:
(a) A reliable basis for taking action and making decisions—'knowledge rather than hunch';
(b) Warning signals when things are going wrong;
(c) A means of delegating the performance of duties and tasks to subordinates. (Budgets are a well known example.)

The following questions are intended to give you a general indication of the quality and effectiveness of the main information produced and circulated in the company. Detailed features of particular types of information, eg sales analyses for marketing executives, are dealt with in later sections.

(a) Broadly speaking is there adequate information for and corresponding to:

(i) all the main functions of the organisation within the company?
(ii) the various managerial levels of the organisation?
(b) Do executives have adequate information about other organisations, markets, and similar aspects of the environment in which the company operates?
(c) Is the information available to executives:
(i) broadly based ie not derived from a narrow set of financial records, but including information of a statistical nature?
(ii) oriented towards future operations and decisions?
(iii) relevant to the main or key decisions which executives have to make?
(iv) relevant to the key factors which influence the successful operation of the business?
(d) Do executives seem fairly satisfied with the information they receive. In particular:
(i) is it the information which they seem to need to carry out their duties?
(ii) in appropriate circumstances can executives make decisions or take action on the basis of this information?
(iii) are they reasonably satisfied with the accuracy and general reliability of the information?
(iv) do they receive the information in time to take action, make decisions, etc?
(v) are they satisfied with the frequency with which such information is provided?
(vi) is there any important information which they think should be produced (not necessarily for them) and which is not currently produced?
(e) Is the information which is produced within the company easily understood by its recipients. In particular:
(i) is the format clear ie easy on the eye?
(ii) is the presentation as simple as possible ie not cluttered with irrelevant data?
(iii) is the terminology unambiguous and readily understood?
(iv) is the terminology free from excessive jargon?
(v) in your view is the information comprehensive in that it relates to all of the main activities and needs of the recipient?
(f) Does the information which is produced include some sort of yardstick as a basis for comparison. Typical yardsticks are:
(i) budgeted or planned levels;
(ii) current levels (eg current stocks compared with current sales levels);
(iii) past levels;
(iv) potential levels;
(v) levels being achieved by competitors;
(vi) average levels being achieved within the industry or country.

PRODUCTION MANAGEMENT

Communications

Probably much more than any other function within the company, the production function depends on the establishment and operation of efficient lines of communication in order that it can perform well.

The following questions are aimed at assessing the lines of communication established in relation to the production organisation.
(a) Are the following functions co-ordinated and ultimately controlled by a person functioning as a chief production executive:
   (i) production engineering?
   (ii) production planning and control?
   (iii) manufacturing departments?
   (iv) raw material and in-process stores?
   (v) maintenance?
(b) Does there seem to be adequate communication between the design and production departments concerning modification to parts and products?
(c) Does there seem to be adequate consultation between production and sales departments in drawing up sales and production programmes, delivery dates and spares requirements?

Production planning and control

It is the function of production planning and control to plan the delivery of materials, purchased parts, and manufactured parts so that they arrive at the assembly stage in the required manner for assembly into finished products in time to meet delivery commitments.

The following questions are aimed at assessing the operation of the production planning and control function.
(a) Is the production planning department operating within the framework of short-range and long-range goals and objectives in respect of the production function. If yes, are the production planners aware of the opportunities, or constraints, contained within this framework?
(b) Is day-to-day routine production planning carried out within the framework of broad schedules of production requirements and manufacturing capacity?
(c) If the directors and senior executives of the company have laid down limits in respect of inventory levels, unit costs, and similar matters, are the production planners aware of these limits and in carrying out their routine planning activities do they attempt to ensure that they keep within these limits?
(d) Does the production control department keep records regarding the work centres in each manufacturing department in sufficient detail to enable it, to prepare schedules of the *actual* work load on each work centre, on a day-by-day basis for the following fortnight or so, and of the *planned* load on each work centre week by week for the next three to six months?
(e) Is there a satisfactory paperwork system for conveying information to manufacturing departments?
(f) Are there procedures for progressing work through every stage within the factory and, where necessary, 'progress chasing' the work?
(g) Do progress chasers appear to work within laid down procedures and disciplines within the factory or do they have to disregard these if they are to get the work out on time?

Inventory control

The maintenance of stocks of materials and parts is necessary in most manufacturing systems. There are many reasons why such stocks have to be held but primarily they are needed to ensure continuity of supply on the factory floor and to enable manufacturing to be carried out in an economic manner.

The following questions should be asked in connection with such systems.
(a) Is there an inventory controller, responsible for the level of stocks held and for the service provided to customers?
(b) In controlling and accounting for the various types of stock, is distinction made between items such as raw materials, manufactured parts, purchased parts, finished goods and spares?
(c) Is there a formal and comprehensive system for recording the movements of stock into and out of stores on records such as bin cards, stock record cards, stock ledger cards, etc?
(d) Are there systematic procedures, based on scientific methods where appropriate, for:
(i) estimating or forecasting short-term future demand for products?
(ii) clearly defining and setting safety stocks, provided as a buffer against variations in planned or anticipated demand or supply?
(iii) calculating economic order quantities (for your purpose you need only know that an economic order quantity is derived from a simple mathematical formula, the parameters of which are the costs associated with carrying inventory and the costs associated with setting up production runs)?
(iv) taking into account stock allocated for special purposes, or to special customers, and for taking into account overdue orders?
(e) Are replenishment orders scrutinised before being issued, at least on a sample basis?
(f) If financial information regarding stock levels is summarised in the periodical accounts, are the various types of stock previously mentioned shown separately?
(g) Are movements in the levels of stock monitored against budgeted levels?
(h) Are there methods or procedures for projecting the value stocks in order that cash flows may be calculated?

Delivery performance

An important method of assessing the effectiveness of the whole production operation is to enquire about the delivery performance that it achieves.

The main questions in respect of delivery performance are:
(a) Is there an important executive, whether he be on the sales or production side, who has a continuing overall picture of the company's delivery promises and delivery commitments?
(b) Are there formal procedures for recording delivery promises and commitments in a comprehensive manner?
(c) Are delivery times reviewed regularly to take account of the size of the order book and any capacity limitations?
(d) Do the delivery times quoted by the company compare favourably with those of its main competitors. Do the delivery times actually achieved compare similarly?

(e) Does the company usually meet its delivery dates?
(f) Are there procedures for recording failures to meet delivery dates and the reasons for such failures?
(g) Are these records summarised and periodically reported to the relevant managers as part of a delivery statistics report?
(h) Do these managers appear to take corrective action if they receive such delivery statistics reports?

Purchasing

It is part of the responsibility of a production controller or an inventory controller to trigger off the raising of orders for parts which are necessary in order to fulfil overall production or stock replenishment programmes. However, it is the buyer's function to purchase the parts and to ensure that this is done as economically as possible.

The following questions are aimed at assessing the effectiveness of any purchasing departments within the company.
(a) Is the purchasing manager consulted by the design office during the product development stage?
(b) Has the company avoided dependence on only one supplier for a key component or components?
(c) In negotiating prices with suppliers, particularly as regards basic raw materials and components having a high annual usage (in cost terms) does the purchasing department project the effect any increases in the prices of these materials and components will have on the profits of the company?
(d) Is the purchasing department free to suggest substitute materials should it experience difficulties in obtaining specified materials, because of delivery delays, excessive price increases, and similar reasons?

Labour control

The following questions are aimed at assessing how well the company is controlling its labour force in order to achieve a balanced maximum output.
(a) Are there procedures for recording labour attendance at the factory?
(b) Are there procedures for recording the actual times spent by individual operatives on individual jobs?
(c) As regards operatives non-productive time:
(i) are there procedures for recording and analysing such time by individual operatives in each department?
(ii) is the total non-productive time further analysed, by department if necessary, into major categories, such as waiting for materials, waiting for machines to be set up, etc?
(iii) is a regular and frequent (preferably daily in many industries) report produced regarding this time and is it circulated to the supervisors and managers in charge of the various manufacturing sections and departments?
(d) As regards the working of overtime:
(i) is such overtime worked on an occasional basis or is it a regular practice to work overtime and something which the operatives expect to do in order to supplement their earnings?

(ii) is the working of overtime authorised by a senior production manager or is it left to each individual operative to work overtime as and when he wants to do so?
(iii) are regular reports provided to supervisors and managers regarding the amount of overtime worked by each man in their departments?
(e) If there is an incentive scheme in operation in the factory, is it achieving the objectives for which it was established as regards achieving certain levels of output?

MARKETING

Introduction

The marketing function has a role to play which is more than just selling or distributing or advertising, for example, the company's products. In its broadest sense marketing is concerned with determining consumers' wants and selecting and fulfilling those which will achieve the company's objectives.

It is essential that the company should have a strong marketing orientation ie it must keep fully aware not only of its customers' requirements and the way in which they are changing or may change, but also of any other emergent trends in the markets in which the company operates.

Market planning and development

Since marketing is concerned with a dynamic, rather than a static, environment it is vital that proper planning is carried out in order to keep abreast of any changes, or emergent trends, in market requirements or conditions.

The following questions should be considered in assessing the effectiveness of the company's planning procedures in respect of its marketing function.
(a) Are there formal established planning procedures in respect of the marketing function?
(b) Are these plans, if any, fully utilised by marketing managers as key control documents as opposed to statements of policy or declarations of intent. Do the plans contain annual sales targets and revenue budgets which should form part of the company's overall budgeting system and, in the case of the sales targets, the annual production plan?
(c) Is marketing research being carried out, either within the company, or through a specialised outside agency, in order to ascertain changing and emergent trends in market requirements and conditions?
(d) Is sufficient consideration being given to longer term marketing development and diversification, by planning more than one year ahead?
(e) Are detailed sales forecasts produced?
(f) Are longer term forecasts prepared for market development and planning purposes and are these generally accepted and utilised by other functions such as production and finance?
(g) Are modern sales forecasting techniques used and if not should their application be considered?
(h) Is time and efford devoted to considering and analysing competitors' activities?

Distribution and product availability

In order to market effectively, and therefore competitively, it is important that the best possible service should be provided for customers, having regard for the cost of the service. This aspect of marketing embraces not only the physical distribution and availability of the company's products but also the choice of the most effective and economic means of reaching the end consumer.

The following questions should help you to assess the company's arrangements for getting its products to its customers.
(a) Is the company fully aware of the distribution pattern of its customers and of the numbers, types and sizes of outlets?
(b) Are the existing distribution channels regularly evaluated in order to determine whether they are the most effective means of reaching the end customer?
(c) When the need arises to provide new warehousing or storage capacity, or to modernise existing facilities, are proper location and cost minimisation studies undertaken before a final decision is made?
(d) Are sufficient finished goods stock levels maintained at suitable locations to meet customer delivery requirements?

Advertising and public relations

Advertising and public relations are highly specialised parts of the overall marketing concept and it is difficult to evaluate the effectiveness of the effort and money expended on publicity, promotion, public relations, and other activities forming a part of the advertising and public relations function.

The following broad questions should be considered however.
(a) Is advertising and public relations expenditure planned on an objective and systematic basis?
(b) Are advertising and sales programmes co-ordinated in order to achieve maximum impact?
(c) Are any serious attempts made to measure in the effectiveness of advertising and publicity programmes. Is any special research undertaken or commissioned for this purpose?
(d) Are competitors' advertising and promotional activities regularly monitored and assessed?

PERSONNEL MANAGEMENT

Manpower planning

The following questions concern the effectiveness with which the company carries out manpower planning.
(a) Has the company attempted to assess its manpower needs over the next 5, 10 and 15 years?
(b) Has it taken appropriate steps to avoid any obvious 'management gaps' which are likely to arise over the next 5, 10 or 15 years?
(c) Has the company attempted to assess its *present* strengths and

weaknesses as regards its manpower, particularly its middle-level and senior executives?
(d) Has the company attempted to assess its *potential* strengths and weaknesses as regards its manpower?
(e) Has it attempted to relate its present and potental strengths and weaknesses to its future manpower needs?
(f) Does the company have the ability and the necessary resources to set up and maintain training and management development programmes appropriate to its anticipated manpower needs?
(g) Does the company have a sufficiently good image and reputation to enable it to recruit outsiders in an effective and lasting manner in order to help satisfy its anticipated manpower needs?

Responsibility for personnel management

The following questions are directed at assessing whether proper responsibility, appropriate to the company's size, complexity and needs, has been established for the management of personnel.
(a) Are the company's personnel problems of sufficient importance to warrant their full time attention by a top level executive, or board member, and if so, is there such an executive or director functioning in this capacity?
(b) If there is no top level executive or board member responsible for personnel management are the company's personnel clear as to who is responsible for personnel?
(c) Has there been any conflict between managers as to who is responsible for personnel management?
(d) If there is a personnel department within the company is it functioning in a comprehensive manner?
(e) If there is a personnel department in the company does it have a clear set of objectives and are sufficient resources allocated to it, in its budget, to enable it to achieve these objectives?

Personnel procedures

The following questions should indicate how well personnel procedures have been established.
(a) Have appropriate procedures been established for the selection, recruitment and engagement of staff. For example:
(i) are objective criteria applied when selecting staff?
(ii) have proper correspondence procedures been established for use when recruiting?
(iii) when engaging staff are there procedures to ensure that the contract of service and conditions of employment are properly understood by the person being engaged?
(b) Once staff have been engaged, are there proper induction procedures to ensure that they are able to take up their duties speedily and with a minimum of disruption to the organisation generally?
(c) Are the procedures for wage and salary administration reasonably simple and efficient?

(d) Are there procedures for the regular and reasonably frequent appraisal of all personnel within the company?

Industrial relations

In most companies operating in developed regions the relations between the company and its work force are a major consideration.

The following questions assess briefly the extent to which proper industrial relations have been established.
(a) Is the company's record on industrial relations over the past few years good in comparison with industrial relations in the industry generally or in the country as a whole?
(b) If the company's record has not been good have steps have been taken to discover the causes for this poor record and in particular have steps been taken to establish conditions and procedures aimed at improving the record?
(c) In your view are the directors, or the personnel department, paying sufficient attention to matters concerned with industrial relations. Furthermore, are the directors or personnel officers sufficiently experienced in dealing with industrial relations and if not are they able to call upon expert advice and assistance when required?
(d) Are directors, executives, managers and personnel officers fully conversant with all the legislation relating to industrial relations?
(e) Are there adequate and realistic collective bargaining procedures which are respected and adhered to in practice?
(f) Following on from the previous question are there formal joint consultation procedures in operation?

FINANCIAL MANAGEMENT

Introduction

This section, on financial management, poses questions of a technical nature for consideration under the following main headings:
(a) Financial planning;
(b) Budgeting;
(c) Financial reporting;
(d) Costing;
(e) Accounting procedures.

Financial planning

Financial planning is primarily concerned with the evaluation in financial terms of the long-term plans and objectives of the company. It is also concerned with setting out and appraising the financial consequences of various courses of action which the company may wish to take.

The following questions should be considered when assessing the quality of the company's financial planning.

(a) Is any form of systematic financial planning being carried out (covering a period beyond that of the normal operating budget)?
(b) If financial planning is being carried out, is this being done in co-operation with all of the executives of the company, or is planning being carried out as an isolated exercise within the finance department?
(c) Is financial planning co-ordinated with and part of a broader strategic plan?
(d) If plans are produced are they in broad harmony with the company's objectives and with other major plans which may have been produced, eg for production and marketing?
(e) Are the financial plans comprehensive in that:
(i) they cover all main operations and activities of the company?
(ii) they include plans in respect of:
1 product turnover and profitability?
2 cost of production?
3 'below the line' expenses?
4 working capital with particular regard to cash flow and inventory levels?
5 capital expenditure?
6 the requirement, if any, for short- and long-term capital funds?
7 the disposal of surplus funds?
(f) In preparing financial plans does the company apply consistent criteria and operate systematic procedures for the review, appraisal and evaluation of:
(i) capital projects?
(ii) research, design and development projects?
(iii) development of new markets?
(g) Are financial plans used:
(i) as a basis for making immediate or short-term decisions. That is, are they translated into action programmes?
(ii) as bench-marks against which actually performance can be measured and reported so that corrective action can be taken, if necessary?

Budgeting

The following questions should be considered in assessing whether the company operates an effective system of budgeting.
(a) Are budgets prepared regularly for use by the executives and managers of the Company?
(b) Is the budgeting process of the company such that executives and managers are able to prepare budgets in respect of their own operations and activities and have them agreed, ultimately, by the board of directors?
(c) Are the budgets agreed in good time, that is well before the commencement of the budget period?
(d) If a budget committee exists does it play an effective role in the budgeting process?
(e) Are budgets fully integrated with long-term financial and other plans, if any?

(f) Are the budgets comprehensive in that all of the company's operations and activities are covered within them?
(g) Are the budgets used as bench-marks against which the actual performance of executives and managers is measured and reported?
(h) If the company's operations and activities can be subject to significant seasonal and other fluctuations, is provision made for adjusting budgets during the budget period in order that variances between budgeted and actual performance may be meaningful when reported?

Financial reporting

The following questions should be considered when assessing the adequacy of the financial reporting system of the company.
(a) Is the distribution of the financial reports comprehensive?
(b) Are financial reports prepared with sufficient frequency for corrective action, if required, to be taken?
(c) Is the system of reporting such that no major areas of the company's operations or activities are ignored?
(d) Are the reports fully integrated so that the summary reports provided for the board and senior executives are supported by, and referenced to, the more detailed reports provided for junior executives, managers and supervisors?
(e) Do the periodic reports include a summarised profit statement and balance sheet?
(f) Are sound and systematic procedures operated for the calcuation and reporting of:
   (i) the gross trading profits?
   (ii) accruals and prepayments?
   (iii) the value of stock and work in progress?
(g) Are the stocks and work in progress shown in the books of account and periodically reported, checked against physical stocks and work in progress at reasonable intervals?
(h) Are significant discrepancies found at stock taking which require material adjustment to be made to the profits reported in the periodical accounts?
(i) At the end of the last financial year were the financial reports for that year in broad agreement with the audited accounts for the year. If there were significant differences between the financial reports and the audited accounts were these due to deficiencies in the method of preparing the financial reports?

Costing

A company will normally operate a costing system for three main purposes. These are:
(a) To provide an accurate means of calculating the profit reported in the company's periodical accounts.
(b) To provide a means for the detailed control of production costs and production efficiency.
(c) To provide cost data concerning the company's products, operations,

and activities which can be used by management in making various decisions.

In reviewing a company's costing system it is therefore necessary to assess to what extent these three requirements are being met. It should be noted that not every company will need a detailed costing system for each of three purposes noted above.

The following questions should help to assess the adequacy of the costing system.

(a) Is the costing system fully integrated with the company's financial records?
(b) Is the distribution of the main periodic costing reports comprehensive and sufficiently frequent?
(c) In determining selling prices is reference made to product costs derived from the costing system; and are these costs found to be helpful and reliable for this purpose?
(d) If it is necessary for costs to be compiled for quotation purposes:
(i) is there a feed-back of actual costs compared with the costs used for quotation purposes?
(ii) Are the cost rates used in quoting reviewed, and if necessary revised, frequently enough?
(e) Is the marginal (direct) costing approach used in fixing selling prices?
(f) Does the costing system enable the profitability of different products to be ascertained?
(g) Would the costing system enable a reliable assessment to be made of the effect on the company's trading results of changes in the following:
(i) sales volume?
(ii) mix of products sold?
(iii) selling prices?
(iv) marginal (direct) costs?
(v) overhead expenditure?
(h) Does the costing system provide useful data to assist management in the following:
(i) the selection of economic manufacturing equipment?
(ii) the most profitable use of surplus manufacturing capacity?
(iii) the allocation of orders to different manufacturing units?
(iv) the choice of manufacturing methods?
(v) the decision on whether to make a product or to buy it?
(i) Does the costing system provide reliable means for evaluating stocks and work in progress:
(i) at the end of the company's financial year?
(ii) for preparation of periodical accounts during the year?
(j) Does the costing system provide a reliable means for calculating gross profit for inclusion in the periodical accounts?
(k) Are there procedures for providing the managers and supervisors responsible for controlling labour costs with periodical reports on the following:
(i) actual productive labour costs incurred on completed work compared with an estimated or standard labour cost?
(ii) non-productive labour costs, such as the cost of labour waiting for work, compared with budget?
(l) Are there procedures for providing the managers and supervisors

responsible for controlling material usage and material costs with periodical reports on the following:
(i) actual costs for materials purchased compared with estimated or standard purchase price?
(ii) the cost of materials actually used in production compared with the estimated or standard costs?
(iii) the cost of materials and finished, or part finished, products which are scrapped during production?
(m) If there is a standard costing system in operation:
(i) are labour standards based on the results of work study exercises?
(ii) are material standards derived from detailed product specifications?
(iii) are standards agreed with the appropriate executives, who are responsible for controlling actual costs against these standards, before being introduced?
(iv) are there procedures for systematically and regularly reviewing and, if necessary, revising standards?
(v) in your view have the standard cost rates been revised sufficiently frequently, and are they now realistic and up-to-date?

Accounting procedures

The company's basic accounting procedures must be reliable.
Some of the major points to be considered when reviewing the accounting procedures are:
(a) Is there an accounting manual. If yes:
(i) does its cover all of the main accounting procedures?
(ii) is the manual reviewed, and if necessary revised, frequently and regularly?
(b) is the accounting work up-to-date or is there a backlog of work relating to any of the main accounting procedures. If there is such a backlog, are realistic and urgent steps being taken to reduce the backlog and is consideration being given to the establishment of procedures for the control of work flow in the accounting department and the elimination, wherever possible, of backlogs of work?
(c) Are all of the accounting records balanced regularly?
(d) Are there weaknesses in accounting procedures (indicated, eg by large differences frequently being found during balancing routines)?
(e) Has the company made a systematic and comprehensive review of the benefits to be obtained from mechanisation of its accounting procedures?
(f) If all or some of the accounting procedures are mechanised do you consider that these procedures are being operated efficiently, within the cost limits set; and that original or current objectives with regard to the mechanisation of the procedures are being achieved?

2.3 Illustration of the contents of a long-form report

TABLE OF CONTENTS

Introduction

Summary of Principal Conclusions and Salient Features

History and Ownership

Nature of Business

    General description
    Purchasing
    Manufacturing
    Selling
    Premises
    Plant
    Financial management
    Management
    Other employees

Trading results

Net Assets

    Summary
    Property, plant and equipment
    Trade investments
    Patents and trade marks
    Goodwill
    Stocks and work in progress
    Debtors and prepayments
    Marketable investments, deposits
    Bank and cash balances
    Bank borrowings
    Creditors, provisions and guaratees
    Taxation

Capital Employed

    Share capital and reserves
    Debentures, long term mortgages

Future Prospects

Taxation, Legal and other Matters

INTRODUCTION

The introduction should include the following matters as a minimum:
(a) Confirmation of the client's instructions (it may be appropriate to attach a copy of the engagement letter as an appendix to the report).
(b) Scope of work undertaken (indicating whether or not any audit work or verification has been done).
(c) Period reviewed and whether auditors have reported without qualification throughout; details of any material qualification should be given.
(d) Sources of information.
(e) Any limitations placed on the investigation (eg where there has been no access to the subject company's officials, or only limited access).
(f) Any major qualifications to the amounts shown later in the report.

SUMMARY OF PRINCIPAL CONCLUSIONS AND SALIENT FEATURES

It is often helpful to summarise the main conclusions at the beginning of the report so that the addressee's attention is drawn to them.

HISTORY AND OWNERSHIP

(a) When, where and by whom established.
(b) Changes of ownership since inception.
(c) When formed into a limited company.
(d) Brief description of capital structure; analysis of major shareholders.

NATURE OF BUSINESS

General description

(a) Nature of original business, subsequent developments, introduction of new products.
(b) Whether the business is dependent on a high level of research and development activity.
(c) General nature of current operations, principal products etc.
(d) Trade reputation.
(e) Structure of group, subsidiary companies, overseas interests etc.
(f) Dates of any special trade agreements.
(g) Future plans, proposed new products, research and development.
(h) Names of principal competitors.

Purchasing

(a) Raw materials used, principal suppliers, origin of supplies, whether prices are comparatively stable or volatile.

(b) Terms of purchases, any significant forward purchase commitments.
(c) The supply position of raw material generally, any difficulties experienced in the past in obtaining requirements either from its regular suppliers or from alternative sources.
(d) If purchases are made from overseas concerns, the rate of import duty and time taken for delivery.
(e) Any control of prices/supply of raw materials by Government departments or under Trade Association agreements, etc.

Manufacturing

(a) General description of the manufacturing processes.
(b) Brief notes on the estimated capacity of the factory; scope for increasing this, etc.
(c) Nature and amount of work sub-contracted to outside firms; the reasons for this policy.

Selling

The investigating accountant's ability to undertake an appraisal of the technical aspects of the business is limited and comments made should normally be restricted to established facts and uncontroversial opinions. It is often necessary to state the limitations of the review of the technical aspects of the business.

If patents, etc are of major importance they should be discussed. If they are of only minor importance there is little advantage in including their details in the report unless this information has been specifically requested. It is normally not possible to state the latent value of patents, etc without valuing the business as a whole. If, however, evidence of their worth is available, including the worth of patents, etc not valued for balance sheet purposes this should be stated.

(a) A brief overall picture of the selling organisation, sales promotion methods, export methods, distribution, etc
(b) Broad analysis of sales by product, by major customers and between home and export
(c) Particulars of any major contracts unfulfilled
(d) The basis used in fixing selling prices
(e) Any controls on selling prices by Government departments, trade associations, etc
(f) Whether sales are susceptible to changes in fashion.

Premises

(a) Description of main premises; types of construction; freehold or leasehold; whether leased and if so full particulars of leases (including dilapidations clauses, options to renew, rent reviews); general condition and deferred repairs.
(b) The location of factories, administrative and selling offices or depots.
(c) Site areas and floor space; whether there is room for expansion.

Illustration of the contents of a long-form report

(d) Any town planning restrictions or approvals for developing the present sites.
(e) Accessability to road, rail, air, sea, canal transport facilities etc.
(f) Brief particulars of the construction costs of the factory and other premises; dates erected; if purchases by the vendor already constructed, the price paid and original cost if known.
(g) Details of any professional valuations.
(h) Whether or not premises are in a development area.

Plant

(a) Description of the main categories of plant used.
(b) Age and apparent condition of the plant.
(c) Any plant not used or obsolete.
(d) Details of any recent revaluation.
(e) Major plant on order, where from, expected delivery dates.

Management

(Covering particulars of the directors, senior executives.)
(a) Name, age, years of service, qualifications and position held.
(b) Experience before joining the company.
(c) Present salaries and other forms of remuneration.
(d) Details of any service agreements and pension schemes.
(e) Policy adopted for training successors or obtaining new staff to succeed the present executives; whether suitable replacements would be readily available.

Other employees

(a) Number of employees at each main factory and office analysed by departments, full time, part time, outworkers, male/female.
(b) Brief particulars of labour relations with management and unions; strike experience and other disturbances.
(c) Approximate present salaries/rates of pay (time and piece work), analysed over functions. Details of any recent pay awards or wage agreements which would affect future costs, particulars of incentive schemes.
(d) Pension scheme arrangements.
(e) Holiday pay arrangements, welfare services (canteens, sports facilities, etc).
(f) Recruitment policy; general availability of labour; training facilities; industrial training levy.

TRADING RESULTS

This section will usually start with a summary of the results for the period before adjustments, adjustments made, and results after adjustments. This would be supported by appendices giving more detailed tabulations or revenues and costs for the period and would be followed by an explanation of the adjustments made for the purposes of the report. It would go on to discuss and comment on the revenues and costs in detail including:

(a) Sales—levels, trends, order book, long term contracts, appropriate analyses by product and market, etc if not already given under general information, commissions deducted, special discounts given, etc.
(b) Other income—details of royalties, management and technical fees, service fees, rents, dividends on trade and other investments, etc.
(c) Gross profits—analysis by product, division, branch, percentage margin on sales, mode of spreading profit on long term contracts.
(d) Overheads—analyses by main categories, trends, etc.
(e) The company's break-even point.
(f) Depreciation and amortisation—basis, rates, treatment of investment grants, position where revaluations have been made.
(g) Treatment of intercompany profits, charges, etc.
(h) Taxation—stock appreciation relief obtained, etc.
(i) Appropriations—dividends on all classes of capital, whether reasonable or, in case of working proprietors, taken as remuneration, cover for dividends, any other appropriations during the period.

NET ASSETS

This section would normally start with a summary of the net assets at the latest balance sheet date and be followed by information as below:

Fixed assets

Property, plant and equipment

(a) Summary of cost and depreciation of main categories.
(b) Particulars of any recent professional valuations, if not already given under general information.
(c) Basis adopted of providing for depreciation/amortisation of each main category.
(d) Review of depreciation rates used compared with other similar businesses.
(e) Any recent changes in the basis of providing depreciation.
(f) Apparent state of maintenance.
(g) Comparison of net book values and tax written down values of assets eligible for capital allowances.
(h) Capital commitments at the balance sheet date and of any significant individual orders placed since.
(i) Insured values and terms of insurance generally.
(j) Treatment of investment grants.
(k) Basis for capitalising own labour and materials.
(l) Arrangements concerning company cars, their private use, etc.

Trade investments

(Including associated companies.)
(a) Date purchased; particulars of holding; percentage of equity held.
(b) General review of income earned.
(c) General review of underlying assets and attributable profits obtained from latest accounts.
(d) Present market values; recent directors' valuations.
(e) Type of business; names of directors and major shareholders if relevant.

Patents and trade marks

(a) Particulars of important patents, trade marks, designs, secret processes. Details of registration, life, etc.
(b) Basis adopted for writing off the capital cost.

Goodwill

How acquired, cost, amounts written of, current value.

Stocks and work in progress

(a) Detail of the basis adopted for valuing stocks.
(b) Basis used in arriving at stock quantities.
(c) How stock quantities have been verified and particulars of procedures in force.
(d) Methods adopted for providing for slow-moving and obsolete stocks, adequacy of provisions.
(e) Rate of turnover.

Debtors and prepayments

(a) Analysis of the age of trade debts.
(b) Approximate number of accounts; details of any major balances.
(c) Usual terms of credit given.
(d) Details of the bad debt provision and bad debt experience.
(e) Credit control methods and policy.
(f) If business is engaged in hire purchase trading, the basis adopted for taking profits on open contracts.
(g) Details of other main receivables.
(h) Dates of redemption of short term loans and rate of interest receivable.

Marketable investments, deposits

(a) Particulars of holdings and market values.
(b) Details including surrender values of insurance policies held.
(c) Details of income received.
(d) Terms of withdrawal or repayment.

Bank and cash balances

Summary of main items.
(a) Details of bank overdraft facilities given as at the balance sheet date and subsequently.
(b) Rate of interest charged.
(c) Details of security given both at the balance sheet date and at present.

Creditors, provisions and gurantees

(a) Approximate number of trade accounts; details of larger balances.
(b) Names of main suppliers.
(c) Usual period credit is allowed or taken; whether this has been normally adhered to over the period covered in the report.
(d) Analysis of other major items.
(e) Details of main movements in the provisions during the period.
(f) Hire purchase agreements.
(g) Guarantees, contingent liabilities, discounted bills, litigation pending.

Taxation

(a) Particulars of liabilities; stages reached in negotiation with the Inland Revenue.
(b) Particulars of important matters in dispute.
(c) Comments on adequacy of overall provision; estimated deficiency or surplus.
(d) Details of losses and allowances available to carry forward and of any available reliefs not yet taken.
(e) Any special wear and tear allowances being claimed.
(f) Basis adopted for calculating deferred tax liabilities.
(g) Any stock appreciation relief claimed and the treatment thereof.
(h) Additional UK liability if accumulated overseas profits are remitted.
(i) Shortfall position.

CAPITAL EMPLOYED

Share capital and reserves

(a) Summary of current authorised and issued share capital.
(b) Rights of each class as to dividends, votes, liquidation, redemption, etc.
(c) Arrears of preference dividend.
(d) Share option schemes.
(e) Particulars of share premium accounts, capital and other reserves.

Debentures, long term mortgages and loans

(a) Amount of borrowing powers.
(b) Rates of interest.

(c) Security granted.
(d) Date of repayment and any sinking fund provisions.

FUTURE PROSPECTS

Where appropriate this section of the report would normally start with a summary of the profit and cash flow forecasts and the assumptions on which these are based. It might then include:
(a) Comment on the assumption and bases used.
(b) Comment on factors which might affect the forecast.
(c) Comment on long term prospects and discussion of any known significant changes since last audited accounts.
(d) Broad details of work done on forecast.
(e) Comment on adequacy of working capital.

TAXATION, LEGAL AND OTHER MATTERS

The sort of matters which typically might be dealt with under this heading might include:
(a) Risk and liability to income or capital transfer tax.
(b) Close company position.
(c) Dividend stripping and depreciatory transactions.
(d) Indemnities recommended from vendors.
(e) Unusual items in memorandum or articles of association.
(f) Contingent liabilities to balancing allowances and capital gains tax.
(g) Steps necessary to maintain continuity of trade for tax losses.
(h) Summary of any matters recommended to be referred to clients' solicitors (deeds, etc).
(i) Any Stock Exchange requirements.
(j) The adequacy of insurance cover generally, including loss of profits.
(k) Confirmation, by reference to file at company registration office, that all requisite documents appear to have been filed.
(l) Availability of interim management accounts, budgets, etc.
(m) Material contracts in the past two years other than in the normal course of business.
(n) A ready reference of names of auditors, solicitors, bankers, brokers, etc.

Chapter 3

Profit Forecasts

INTRODUCTION	3.01
TECHNICAL REQUIREMENTS	3.02
Definition of profit forecast	3.02
Publication of a profit forecast	3.06
Responsibility of the directors	3.11
Responsibility of the reporting accountants	3.16
Responsibility of the financial advisers	3.21
Requirements of the City Code	3.26
Requirements of The Stock Exchange	3.36
The features of a profit forecast	3.43
ORGANISING THE WORK	3.62
The preliminary review	3.62
Obtaining detailed written instructions	3.71
Planning	3.72
FIELDWORK	3.75
General	3.75
Review of method of preparation	3.76
Testing the reliability of forecasts	3.78
Detailed examination of forecasts	3.80
Results achieved to date	3.81
Working capital forecasts	3.82
DOCUMENTATION	3.83
REPORTING	3.84
Publishing short-form reports	3.84
Published financial advisers' reports	3.87
Consent to publish	3.91
Consent to the extended use of forecasts	3.92
Unpublished long-form reports	3.93

72 *Profit forecasts*

PRACTICAL GUIDES

City Code on take-overs and mergers: Practice Note 6	3.1
City Code on take-overs and mergers: Practice Note 7	3.2
Profit and working capital forecast review: specimen letter of engagement	3.3
Profit and working capital forecast review: aide-memoire	3.4
Profit and working capital forecast review: specimen working papers	3.5
Profit and working capital forecast review: specimen short-form reports	3.6
Profit and working capital forecast review: illustration of the contents of an unpublished long-form report	3.7
Profit and working capital forecasts: forecasting working papers	3.8

INTRODUCTION

3.01 This chapter describes the situation in which the investigating accountant may be requested to prepare a report on a profit forecast, the requirements which must be satisfied in doing this, and the work involved.

TECHNICAL REQUIREMENTS

Definition of a profit forecast

3.02 The Institute of Chartered Accountants in England and Wales in their Members Handbook section 3.918 define a profit forecast as:

> 'any published estimate of financial results that is made for any one or more of the following:
> (a) in advance of the completion of financial statements up to publication standard for any expired accounting period;
> (b) for a current (or unexpired) accounting period;
> (c) for a future accounting period'.

This definition extends to certain statements that are not expressed in terms of figures (eg 'profits will be somewhat higher than last year').

3.03 Care must be taken to ensure that all parties concerned know what is meant by a profit forecast as opposed to a profit target or some other form of budget. A profit forecast is the level of profitability that the directors reasonably and honestly expect to achieve, whereas a profit target might represent the profit level to which management may be striving. A budget may have been adopted by the directors for particular management use in the circumstances of the company, and it may not be a profit forecast. In arriving at a forecast the directors will have to make certain assumptions which are those matters over which the directors are unable to exercise control but which, if they prove to be incorrect, can materially upset the forecast.

3.04 The City Code also puts a strict interpretation on what constitutes a forecast. A statement need not include figures in order to be a forecast. Practice Note No 6, paragraph 7 states

> 'It should be appreciated that even when no particular figure is mentioned certain forms of words may constitute a profit forecast. Examples are "profits will be somewhat higher than last year" and "the profits of the second half year are expected to be similar to those earned in the first half year" (when interim figures have already been published). It is impossible to generalise but broadly whenever a form of words puts a floor under (or, in certain circumstances, a ceiling on) the likely profits of a particular period or whenever a form of words contains the data necessary to ascertain an approximate figure for future profits by an arithmetical process, the panel takes the view that there is a profit forecast

which, except to the extent that in exceptional circumstances specific dispensation has been obtained, must be reported on'.

3.05 The Stock Exchange also puts a strict interpretation on what, in its view, constitutes a profit forecast. In August 1975 the Council of The Stock Exchange issued the following statement:

> 'The Council wish it to be understood that for the purpose of deciding whether a profit forecast has been made the Council will have regard to any words which may be used in commenting either upon future accounting periods, or on past accounting periods for which results have not been announced to the public. Whenever it becomes possible, by using such words in conjunction with published data, to arrive at an approximate figure for future profits by an arithmetical process, the Council will take the view that a forecast has been made and require it to be reported upon in accordance with Appendix 34.
>
> The Council have also decided that if there is in existence any profit in respect of an unexpired accounting period, or period which has expired but for which results have not been announced to the public, a statement should be made in any prospectus confirming, amending, or withdrawing such forecast. Where appropriate, reports will then be required'.

Publication of a profit forecast

3.06 There are no requirements in the UK for companies or other organisations to make or to publish profit forecasts. If, however, a company has issued a forecast in respect of a particular accounting period, or even has published any statement which is so worded that it might be construed as a profit forecast, and if subsequently the company becomes involved (either willingly or unwillingly) in take-over negotiations or in the issue of a public document, it may be required by The Stock Exchange to confirm or amend that forecast. Also, where appropriate, the company may be required to arrange for an independent report on the forecast.

3.07 Quite apart from this, when boards of directors are communicating either with existing shareholders or with potential future shareholders, there may be circumstances in which they are responsible for providing all the information needed by the recipients to make an informed judgment. In such circumstances, the directors may consider it is necessary to publish a forecast of the probable outcome of the current financial period and sometimes of the succeeding period as well.

3.08 There are three principal situations in which independent accountants may be approached to report on profit forecasts:
(a) When a company proposes to publish a profit forecast in connection with a take-over or a merger that is subject to The City Code on Takeovers and Mergers ('the City Code');
(b) When a company proposes to publish a profit forecast as part of listing

particulars, or an offer for sale, or some other document, the issue of which is subject to the rules and regulations of The Stock Exchange;
(c) When the independent accountants are appointed to carry out an investigation, or a review of a company, or an unincorporated business, and the terms of the accountants' appointment include a review of profit forecasts.

3.09 In the first and second situations outlined above, the accountants would be required to produce a report for publication. This would be a short report which is generally referred to as a 'short-form report'. In the third situation outlined above, the report would be in greater detail and would not be intended for publication. Such reports are, however, frequently required additionally in the first and second situations. Naturally, the accountants may be asked to report orally on their findings.

3.10 In other circumstances, a company's directors may be required to publish in listing particulars a statement that, in their opinion, the working capital available to the company is sufficient, or, how they propose to provide the additional working capital which they consider necessary. In such a case, the issuing house will normally be required to write to the Quotations Department of The Stock Exchange confirming that they have satisfied themselves that the directors' statement has been made after due and careful enquiry. Although such statements do not amount to a formal profit forecast, independent accountants may be commissioned to provide a report supporting the statement issued by the directors and the issuing house. Inevitably such a report must be based on a review of the company's forecast of profit working capital requirements.

Responsibility of the directors

3.11 The profit forecast should represent the directors' best estimate of the results that they believe will be achieved by the company, rather than a desirable target which has been set to inspire performance. There may, however, be a difference of emphasis between a profit forecast issued in a take-over situation (where speed may be imperative, and an over-pessimistic approach may damage the legitimate interests of the company's shareholders), and a profit forecast issued for listing particulars purposes (where speed is not usually so important, but where an over-optimistic forecast that is not achieved may harm shareholders by damaging the company's market status).

3.12 The sole responsibility for a profit forecast rests with the directors who cannot be relieved of their responsibility by reporting accountants or financial advisers who cannot in any way underwrite, or guarantee or otherwise accept responsibility for the ultimate realisation of a forecast.

3.13 The directors must also understand that *in no circumstances* can reporting accountants prepare a profit forecast on behalf of the directors. The preparation of a forecast involves a close working knowledge of all the factors affecting profitability of the business, including the directors' future intentions. As reporting accountants they would not have this knowledge. In exceptional circumstances it may be necessary to assist directors in the preparation of a forecast, but the reporting accountants should first satisfy themselves that it is impossible for the company to undertake this work unaided and should explain to the directors that the ultimate responsibility for the forecast is theirs alone.

3.14 Naturally, compilation of a forecast will be delegated to management and staff. When this is done, however, directors must recognise that forecasting requires the exercise of skill and judgment in projecting future likely events and they should carefully determine how much responsibility each person will be taking, so that they know, without doubt, which individuals will account to them for different parts of the forecast. Everyone involved should be properly briefed about the assumptions which are to be used in preparing the detailed forecast and should appreciate the degree of judgment which may be exercised. When prepared, the staff responsible for compiling the forecasts should explain them in detail to the full board of directors so that the forecast may be accepted as the board's responsibility.

3.15 Finally, before a document containing a profit forecast is despatched, the board of directors should meet to approve the contents of the document. In doing so, the final forecast figures should be explained and the directors should minute specifically their approval of the wording of the forecast and the assumptions on which it is based. Every director should take responsibility for the forecast. The reporting accountants and the financial advisers will normally wish to be present when the board meet for this purpose.

Responsibility of the reporting accountants

3.16 It is not possible for reporting accountants to verify a profit forecast in the same way as they would verify financial statements published in respect of completed accounting periods. There can be no question of auditing a forecast, even though the reporting accountants may also be the company's auditors.

3.17 The City Code requires that 'the accounting policies and calculations for the forecasts must be examined and reported on by the auditors or consultant accountants'. The Stock Exchange uses similar wording in its requirements. It is customary, therefore, for published reports to use this form of wording. This may seem a rather narrow responsibility but the reporting accountants should regard the assumptions on which a profit forecast is based as an integral part of the forecast. The reporting accountants' responsibility is therefore to satisfy themselves that the accounting bases and calculations for the forecast have been properly compiled on the footing of the assumptions made. As a result of their review the reporting accountants should be in a position to advise the company on what assumptions should be listed in stating the forecast, and also on the way in which they should be described. They should satisfy themselves as informed persons, rather than as experts, that the assumptions are realistic in the circumstances, that they are clearly stated in the forecast, and that no significant assumptions have been omitted.

3.18 The reporting accountants should satisfy themselves that the directors have prepared and presented the forecast in a responsible manner, and that it represents the directors' best estimate of the results which they believe will be achieved. In satisfying themselves that the forecast is attainable the reporting accountants should form a judgment on the company's resources, particularly those relating to working capital, raw material suppliers, manpower and management, to ensure that the company will not be prevented from achieving the forecast results by limitations in the available resources. Since listed companies are required to make preliminary profits announcements at least half yearly, such figures are usually a substantial part of any profit forecast made by such a company. The City Code now requires that reporting accountants should report on any unaudited figures published during an offer period.

3.19 Whether or not a public report is required, the reporting accountants should normally prepare, for discussion with the company's directors and with financial advisers, an extended and detailed report on the forecasts. Preparation of such a report ensures that all parties are informed of any relevant facts, provided to the reporting accountants, concerning the preparation of the forecast.

3.20 When the report is to be published in a formal document, both the City Code and The Stock Exchange require the reporting accountants to give their consent to the issue of the document. This is generally interpreted as meaning that the reporting accountants should be satisfied that the document in which their report is to be published is not in any way misleading. Reporting accountants should therefore see all proofs of any such document, and also attend any meetings concerned with the drafting of that document.

Responsibility of the financial advisers

3.21 A company offering to buy the shares of another company will usually employ a merchant banker, or some other licensed dealer, to act as financial adviser and to make the offer on its behalf. If the offeror company issues a profit forecast, the merchant banker, or other licensed dealer involved, would report on the profit forecast as financial adviser.

3.22 The City Code requires the board of an offeree company to obtain competent independent advice on any offer, and also to make the substance of such advice known to its shareholders. Financial advisers cannot act for both the offeror and the offeree at the same time.

3.23 Where a profit forecast is subject to the rules of the City Code or The Stock Exchange, the responsibilities of other financial advisers are laid down. For example, the City Code rule 16 makes the following requirement:

> 'The accounting bases and calculations for the forecasts must be examined and reported on by the auditors or consultant accountants. Any financial adviser mentioned in the document must also report on the forecasts. The accountants' report and, if there is an

adviser, his report, must be contained in such document and be accompanied by a statement that the accountants and, where relevant, the adviser have given and not withdrawn their consent to publication'.

3.24 A duty is also placed on the financial advisers to discuss the forecast assumptions with their client, and to satisfy themselves that it has been prepared with scrupulous care and objectivity. They are also required to ensure that no assumption is published that appears to them to be unrealistic. If interim unaudited profit figures are published during the offer period the financial advisers must also report on them.

3.25 In theory, it can be argued that the responsibility of the reporting accountants is more limited than is that of the financial advisers. In practice, it will be found that both the reporting accountants and the financial advisers require to be satisfied that the forecast represents the results that the directors honestly believe will be achieved. They will also require to be satisfied that the forecast is fairly presented.

Requirements of the City Code

3.26 The City Code on Take-overs and Mergers is issued on the authority of the Council of the Securities Industry and General Principle No 3 states:

> 'Shareholders shall have in their possession sufficient evidence, facts and opinions upon which an adequate judgment and decision can be reached, and shall have sufficient time to make an assessment and decision. No relevant information shall be withheld from them'.

3.27 Although this implies that it may be desirable to publish a profit forecast in the context of a take-over offer, it does not specifically require that there should be one, and if the directors believe they can give adequate up-to-date information by other means they are permitted to do so. In particular, if they believe that forecasting is hazardous they should be dissuaded from publishing forecasts other than for expired, or mainly-expired, periods.

3.28 The Code lays particular emphasis on the need for care to be exercised when profit forecasts are prepared and published. General Principle No 12 of the Code states:

> 'Any document or advertisement addressed to shareholders containing information, opinions or recommendations from the board of an offeror or offeree company or their respective advisers shall be treated with the same standards of care as if it were a prospectus within the meaning of the Companies Act 1948. Especial care shall be taken over profit forecasts'.

This general principle is re-emphasised in rule 16 of the Code, which states:

> 'Without in any way detracting from the necessity of maintaining the

highest standards of accuracy and fair presentation in all communications to shareholders in a take-over or merger transaction, attention is particularly drawn in this connection to profit forecasts and asset valuations.'

and also states:

'Notwithstanding the obvious hazard attached to the forecasting of profits, any profit forecasts must be compiled with the greatest possible care by the directors whose sole responsibility they are'.

3.29 When a profit forecast is included in any circular to shareholders in connection with an offer, rule 16 of the Code makes the following requirements:
(a) the company's auditors or consultant accountants must examine and report on the accounting policies and the calculations for the forecast;
(b) any financial adviser mentioned in the document must also report on the forecasts;
(c) the accountants' report and (if there is an adviser) the adviser's report, must be contained in the document, and it must be accompanied by a statement that those making the reports have given their consent to the reports being published, and they have not withdrawn that consent;
(d) the assumptions (including the commercial assumptions) upon which the directors have based their profit forecast must be stated in the document;
(e) wherever a profit forecast appears in relation to a period in which trading has already commenced, profit figures previously published in respect of any expired portion of that trading period, together with comparable figures for the preceding year, must be stated.

3.30 Practice Note No 6 re-emphasises that a profit forecast must be prepared with scrupulous care and objectivity. It lays a duty on financial advisers to satisfy themselves that the forecast has been prepared by the directors in this manner. The financial advisers and the auditors or the consultant accountants are required to assist the directors to make the underlying assumptions as meaningful as possible.

3.31 Any forecast made before the commencement of the offer period must be repeated in the offer document, and it must be examined and reported on. The only exception to this is a forecast made by an offeror making an offer consisting solely of cash. No report is required in respect of such a forecast. Similar requirements do not apply to unaudited statements of annual or interim results that have already been published, but independent accountants are required to report on any unaudited profit figures published during an offer period.

3.32 If a forecast upon which reporting accountants and financial advisers have reported is included in a document, then any subsequent document that the company publishes in connection with the offer must contain a statement by the directors that the forecast remains valid for the purposes of the offer. Subsequent documents must also state that the financial advisers and the accountants who reported on the forecast have indicated that they have no objection to their reports continuing to apply.

80 *Profit forecasts*

3.33 If a forecast is prepared under the current cost convention then it must be accompanied by a corresponding forecast prepared under the historical cost convention. The reporting accountants and the financial advisers must report on both forecasts.

3.34 The Code suggests that the following general rules should apply to the selection and the drafting of assumptions:
(a) the reader should be able to understand the implications of the assumptions, and thus be helped to judge the reasonableness of the forecast and the main uncertainties to which it is subject;
(b) the assumptions should be, wherever possible, specific rather than general, and definite rather than vague;
(c) all-embracing assumptions and assumptions relating to the general accuracy of the estimates should be avoided;
(d) the assumptions should be related only to matters that may have a material bearing on the forecast.

3.35 Practice Notes Nos 6 and 7 of the City Code deal with the above matters in detail (see Practical Guides **3.1** and **3.2**).

Requirements of The Stock Exchange

3.36 The Stock Exchange regulations will be found in the book *Admission of Securities to Listing* (The Stock Exchange Yellow Book), a new edition of which was published in 1984 incorporating changes brought about by the implementation of three new EEC directives. One of the most significant of these changes was the introduction of 'listing particulars' instead of a prospectus for a company seeking a listing for any of its securities. The detailed requirements relating to listing particulars are set out in Section 3 of *The Stock Exchange Yellow Book*.

3.37 The Stock Exchange rules require listing particulars to include a statement on the financial and trading prospects of the company or group, together with any material information that may be relevant to an assessment of those prospects. This should include all special trade factors or risks (if any) that are not mentioned elsewhere in the prospectus, and that are unlikely to be known or anticipated by the general public, and that could materially affect profits; Section 3 Chap 2 Pt 7 para 7.1(b).

3.38 This is not in itself a requirement to issue a profit forecast. When, as frequently happens, a forecast is published, The Stock Exchange Rules state:

> 'Where a profit forecast appears in any listing particulars the principal assumptions, including commercial assumptions, upon which the directors have based their profit forecast, must be stated. The accounting policies and calculations for the forecast must be examined and reported on by the reporting accountants, and their report must be set out. The issuing house, or, in the absence of an issuing house, the sponsoring broker must report in addition whether or not they have satisfied themselves that the forecast has

been stated by the directors after due and careful enquiry, and such report must be set out'; Section 3 Chap 2 Pt 7 para 2.

3.39 The requirements for the information that has to be provided before a company can enter the Unlisted Securities Market of The Stock Exchange include almost identical provisions.

3.40 These requirements are similar to those of the City Code although they are, however, more specific as to the contents of the report published by the issuing house or the sponsoring brokers, who are required to report 'whether or not they have satisfied themselves that the forecast has been stated by the directors after due and careful enquiry'. The requirements also require the report to be made by reporting accountants who are independent of the company and any other party to the same degree as is required of auditors under the Companies Acts, whereas the City Code permits the report to be made by 'auditors or consultant accountants'.

3.41 It should be noted, however, that if a company has already published a profit forecast, The Stock Exchange requires that a statement should be made in any listing particulars that either confirms or amends the forecast. Where appropriate, a report by reporting accountants will then be required. Such circumstances might require that a profit forecast be included, and also that a report be made on it in a rights issue document.

3.42 When a company publishes a circular to shareholders in respect of a substantial acquisition it must also comply with the requirements relating to listing particulars specified in Section 6 Chap 1 para 3.5 of *The Stock Exchange Yellow Book*. This applies regardless of whether or not the consideration takes the form of shares or other securities or cash (*The Stock Exchange Yellow Book* Section 6 Chap 1 para 1.3). Such a circular is frequently issued in the form of a document recommending an offer, and it is therefore covered by the requirements of the City Code regarding the publication of profit forecasts in take-over documents. However, if a circular regarding a substantial acquisition is issued purely to inform shareholders after the event has happened, and it does not relate to the sale or issue of securities for which a listing is sought, it may not constitute either listing particulars or a take-over document. Consequently, the rules regarding profit forecasts, either in *The Stock Exchange Yellow Book* or in the City Code, would not apply. In the case of doubt, the company should inform the broker, who should consult the Quotations Department of the Stock Exchange.

The features of a profit forecast

3.43 The important features of a profit forecast are as follows:
(a) the period covered by the forecast;
(b) the form of the published forecast;
(c) the assumptions made in preparing the forecast;
(d) the latest unaudited profit figures (see **3.55**);
(e) the company's normal accounting policies;
(f) follow up.

82 Profit forecasts

The period covered by the forecast

3.44 In normal circumstances, accountants should not undertake to review and report on a profit forecast if it is intended to cover any period beyond the date of expiry of the current accounting period. In exceptional circumstances, independent accountants may agree to report on a forecast for an accounting period that has not yet commenced, eg where a significant part (at least nine months) of the current accounting period has elapsed, or where the directors propose to make a forecast covering only a part of the following accounting period. It should be noted that, for the purposes of the City Code, statements referring to prospects for limited periods (eg the following quarter) will be regarded as falling within the rules and will be subject to the requirements for a forecast covering a full year.

3.45 In some cases, reports on projections for longer periods may be required, eg where listing particulars are issued in connection with an entirely new project or for certain unpublished reports. Special considerations apply in such cases since as the period covered by a forecast is increased, so the implicit uncertainties also increase and the validity of the assumptions on which the forecast is based will be undermined. The considerations appropriate for such work are discussed later in this chapter.

The form of a published forecast

3.46 A published forecast does not necessarily have to be expressed in monetary amounts. For forecasts to be informative, however, it is generally preferable to give monetary amounts, and the majority of forecasts take the form of a pro-forma profit and loss account. City Code Practice Note 6 says that:

> 'there should be included where possible forecasts of turnover, profit before taxation, taxation (when the figure is significantly abnormal), minority interests and extraordinary items (when either of these amounts is material)'.

The Stock Exchange rules do not include specific requirements as to the form of a published forecast. For this reason, forecasts in listing particulars are sometimes restricted to an estimate of 'estimated group profit before taxation'.

3.47 Because of the uncertainties attached to forecasting, directors may choose to publish a range within which the actual profit is considered likely to fall (ie a sensitivity analysis) which may perhaps be accompanied by an assessment of the possibilities associated with the basic assumptions. City Code Practice Note 7 states:

> 'It may be helpful to indicate what the effect on the profit forecast would be if certain of the major assumptions were to prove to be wholly or partly invalid'.

3.48 In some circumstances it may be necessary to specify the bases and the accounting policies adopted in preparing the forecast, if these cannot be ascertained from the accounting policies normally adopted by the company.

3.49 The statement of assumptions should normally be regarded as an essential part of the published forecast. The only exception to this is likely to be where the forecast period has already expired, and it is not necessary to make assumptions about future events.

3.50 In examining a published forecast, the reporting accountants will wish to be satisfied that it shows clearly:
(a) the period for which the forecast is made;
(b) whether it is subject to any major uncertainties that should be disclosed;
(c) whether the principal assumptions on which it is based are clearly stated.

Assumptions used in preparing a forecast

3.51 A profit forecast (whether it is published or not) should state the major assumptions on which it is based. A useful commentary on assumptions will be found in City Code Practice Note 7 (see Practical Guide **3.2**). In determining the assumptions, particular attention should be paid to the general rules set out in that Practice Note. Assumptions are those matters over which the directors are unable to exercise control and which, if they prove to be incorrect, can materially upset a forecast and as such should be distinguished from safeguards. Safeguards are those matters over which the directors have control, and in wishing to state them, are trying only to protect themselves against error or the inaccurate projection of matters that are normally under their control.

3.52 It is the directors' responsibility to make reasonable assumptions about those unknown factors which could materially upset the realisation of their forecasts. These factors will often be determined by the size and the type of the organisation and by the geographical areas in which it trades. For example, political and world economic assumptions may be vital to a large organisation but relatively remote to a small organisation.

3.53 Assumptions should not relate to the accuracy of the accounting and the forecasting systems. Most of the integral parts of a forecast are matters over which the directors have control. Moreover, the forecast is prepared on the basis that the trading and the accounting policies are known factors under the directors' control, and those policies are not likely to be changed while the existing directors exercise control. However, where there is a possibility of a change in the board (as in a take-over), or where a forecast extends to the following financial period, it may be necessary to state as an assumption that there will be no change in existing trading and accounting policies.

3.54 Although reporting accountants have no responsibility for the assumptions, as a result of their review they should be in a position to advise the company both on the assumptions that should be listed in the published document, and on the way in which those assumptions should be described.

The latest unaudited profit figures

3.55 Rule 16 of the City Code requires that when a profit forecast is to be published covering a period which has already commenced, any previously published profit figures in respect of the expired portion of that trading period must be stated, together with comparable figures for the preceding year. If such figures were published before the offer period commenced, independent accountants are not required to report on them. Unaudited profit figures published during an offer period must be reported on by accountants and financial advisers.

3.56 The Stock Exchange rules do not include any requirements regarding interim unaudited figures, other than as to the content and the timing of the issue of interim figures (which are dealt with under 'Continuing Obligations'; Section 5 Chap 2 paras 24 and 25 of *The Stock Exchange Yellow Book*).

3.57 Generally speaking, no unaudited profit figures should be included in an offer document unless they have been prepared with the same standard of care, and carry the same degree of authority, as unaudited interim or preliminary final results published by the company. The dangers of reproducing figures of a lesser standard in a document circulated in the context of a bid outweigh any advantage likely to be gained from doing so.

3.58 A profit forecast rarely includes interim figures unless those figures have been published, but there is no objection to reporting accountants, or other financial advisers, referring in their reports to the fact that in reviewing the forcast they have taken available management figures into account.

The accounting policies normally adopted by the company

3.59 The accountants' report will normally state that the forecast is presented on a basis consistent with the accounting policies normally adopted by the company or the group. These accounting policies should be identifiable within the document in which the forecast is published. If the document is a prospectus, a statement of the accounting policies will be an identifiable section of the accountants' report on the financial affairs of the company (see Chapter 4). If the document is an offer document, information regarding the financial affairs of both the offeror and the offeree are required by the City Code to be included, and such information should include a statement of accounting policies.

3.60 If the accounting policies adopted in preparing the profit forecast are significantly different from those normally adopted by the company, attention should be drawn to that fact both in the presentation of the forecast and in the accountants' report on the forecast.

Follow up

3.61 If any information about a major deviation from a published forecast becomes known to a company, the directors should make this information public as soon as possible after they learn of it. Section 5 of *The Stock Exchange Yellow Book* 'Continuing Obligations', which all companies listed in the UK are required to observe, requires listed companies to circulate, with the annual report of the directors, an explanation (where applicable) of why the results shown by the accounts for the period under review differ materially from any forecast published by the company. This requirement will cover forecasts issued for any purpose, and not merely those published in listing particulars and take-over documents. The Stock Exchange applies a rough guideline that the outturn of a profit forecast should be within 10% of the forecast, and there is a monitoring system to ensure that any greater variation is explained. The Panel on Take-overs and Mergers monitors, on a sampling basis, the profits subsequently reported by companies who have made a forecast in the course of an offer. If a company fails to meet its forecast within a margin of, say, 10% either way, the Panel may investigate the reason for the variation. The Panel may also call for explanations from the company, the reporting accountants and the financial advisers.

ORGANISING THE WORK

The preliminary review

3.62 A request to act as reporting accountants in connection with a profit forecast to be used in either a take-over or a merger that is subject to the City Code can arise unexpectedly at any time, the time available to carry out the work often being short. In addition, the reporting accountant would probably be asked to start work almost immediately.

3.63 On being invited to examine a profit forecast, the accountants responsible should arrange, immediately, to visit the client's headquarters to review the situation and settle the terms of the engagement. Before being able to judge whether to accept the engagement, the reporting accountants will need to know:
(a) the reason why the company proposes to publish the forecast;
(b) the present state of completeness of both the forecast and the underlying accounting records;
(c) the period to be covered by the forecast;
(d) whether the forecast is to be updated especially to meet the present situation;
(e) the date by which the report will be required;
(f) the assumptions that the company expects to make;
(g) whether the forecast will incorporate changes in previous accounting policies;
(h) whether interim unaudited profit figures are likley to be issued before the offer period expires;
(i) the availability of directors and other key executives for discussion on particular aspects of the forecast.

3.64 If the reporting accountants are not the auditors of the company, or have no previous relationship with the company, they will also need to know:
(a) the nature and the background of the company's business;
(b) the structure of the group (where there are subsidiaries or associated companies);
(c) the location of the accounting units;
(d) the accounting policies the company normally follows, and the consistency with which the company applies such policies in subsidiaries and/or branches;

(e) the profit and the cash flow forecasting procedures the company uses, and the reliance that can be placed on interim accounts and costing records;
(f) whether the auditors have qualified their reports in recent years.

3.65 This list is not exhaustive, and as information is made available other questions will invariably arise. Having obtained this information, the accountants should consider whether they are willing to act and, if so, confirm in a letter of engagement their understanding of the instructions. Offer negotiations in which profit forecasts are involved frequently start in great haste, but can drag on for a considerable period. This factor makes it important that the basis of the engagement is agreed with the client company at the commencement.

3.66 In deciding whether to accept an engagement to report on a profit forecast, the independent accountants should consider the following critical matters, all of which are interrelated:
(a) the degree of sophistication of the company's forecasting procedures, including the reliability of previous forecasts, and the adequacy and reliability of its interim accounts;
(b) the period to be covered by the forecast;
(c) the nature of the company's business;
(d) the date by which the accountants' reports are required.

3.67 Firstly, the degree of sophistication of the company's forecasting procedures and the adequacy and reliability of interim accounts are of fundamental importance when the forecast represents a projection for a substantial period, or when it is required in a hurry. If, as in the case of a prospectus, speed is less likely to be immediately critical, and if the forecasting procedures are inadequate, then it is in the long-term interest of the company that such shortcomings should be rectified. A reputable issuing house would not agree to sponsor an issue unless steps were taken to implement satisfactory procedures before preparing a forecast for publication. If, however, timing is critical (as is invariably the case where a company is resisting an unwanted bid), and if the forecasting procedures and the preparation of interim accounts are unsatisfactory, and the company's structure and operations complicated, then the reporting accountants should seriously consider whether they are able to act. Alternatively, they may decide to act, but should indicate to the directors that their report may have to be qualified by reference to the reliability of the forecasting procedures. This applies, particularly, when they do not act as the auditors, and do not have a detailed knowledge of the accounting procedures.

3.68 Secondly, the period to be covered by the forecast may be critical. Accountants should not normally undertake to report publicly on a forecast for more than the current accounting period and (provided that a sufficiently significant part of the current year has elapsed) the next following accounting year. In deciding what is a significant part of the year, they would have regard to the whole situation of the client company. However, the circumstances in which an engagement to report on a period other than the current period is accepted would be exceptional. Consequently, if accountants consider that the period to be covered by the forecast is unreasonable they should decline to act.

3.69 Thirdly, the nature of the business should not be such as to make it almost impossible for the directors to forecast the outcome with any degree of certainty: eg dealing businesses whose profits may be so unpredictable that, even if a substantial part of the forecasting period has elapsed, the final result cannot be foreseen. In such circumstances, the accountants should decline to act, or alternatively should indicate to the directors that their report will probably be qualified by reference to the uncertainties inherent in the business.

3.70 Fourthly, the time within which the report is required should not be so severely restricted that it would be impossible to obtain sufficient information for the purpose of reporting. One of the major differences in practice between a forecast that is required for listing particulars and one that is required for a City Code document is the amount of time that is likely to be available. In the former case, the accountants would probably have a reasonable amount of time in which to complete their work. In a take-over, by contrast, the requirements of the City Code are such that the company may press for a report in a period of two to three weeks, or even less. It is essential that the accountants should nonetheless have sufficient time to carry out their work. If they are unable to agree on what is a reasonable period of time they should decline to act. Alternatively, they should request that the issue of circulars should be deferred.

Obtaining detailed written instructions

3.71 It is important that the reporting accountants should confirm their understanding of the client's instructions in a letter of engagement, at the earliest practicable time. Examples of paragraphs which should be included in such a letter of engagement are set out in Practical Guide 3.3.

Planning

3.72 The reporting accountants should ensure that the standard of judgment applied over the whole engagement is uniform, and adequately brief those who do the detailed work. At the outset they should determine:
(a) the areas of the company's activities that are significant in terms of their contribution both to the forecast results and to previous audited results;
(b) the areas that are likely to give rise to difficulties because of the nature of the activities or because of the economic factors affecting the activities;
(c) the acceptability of the accounting policies that were previously followed, or that are to be followed in the forecast (if these are different from the previous policies);
(d) the reasonableness of the assumptions on which the forecast is to be based, as set out in any instructions the company issues to its accounting locations; and
(e) the extent of the review work which will be necessary. Where the report is intended only to support a statement by financial advisers on the

adequacy of working capital, the extent of their review may be materially affected by the margin of resources over the apparent level of required working capital.

3.73 Once these matters have been determined, the accountants should prepare detailed instructions for staff and any other firms of accountants carrying out specific sections of the work. Such instructions should indicate:
(a) the reasons for a report on the forecast being required;
(b) the date by which the information is required;
(c) the name, the location, the telephone number and the telex number of the partner or the manager who is in charge of the engagement;
(d) the information required to be reported and the manner of the reporting;
(e) the contents of working papers;
(f) the billing arrangements.

3.74 Because the nature of the work requires the exercise of a great deal of judgment, a partner in the firm of accountants reporting on the forecast should be closely involved in the work and it is generally necessary to use experienced staff. Considerable care must be exercised to identify the appropriate people to be involved.

FIELDWORK

General

3.75 As a result of the differing nature of companies' organisations, procedures and businesses, it is impracticable to specify a standard programme of the work to be undertaken. However, it is helpful to adopt a systematic approach and to this end Practical Guide **3.4** sets out in the form of an aide-memoire matters to be considered during the various stages of the profit forecast review. It should be emphasised that these are not exhaustive lists of questions or considerations, but are intended only as a guide. Each section of the work as set out in the aide-memoire is considered in turn below.

Review of method of preparation

3.76 The purpose of this part of the review is to establish the general nature of the company's activities, its main products, markets, customers, suppliers, divisions, labour force and trend of results. The sources of information will include audit permanent files and final notes, current management accounts and budgets, copies of long form and other reports issued on the business, discussions with the company's officials and merchant bankers, and an examination of the minutes of the board, and where appropriate, committee meetings. In addition, the reporting accountants should ascertain the company's method of preparing the forecast. If forecasting is a procedure normally undertaken by the company and not an ad hoc exercise, the established basis of preparation can be examined. It is probable in the former case that the forecast will be based on departmental or divisional budgets which are co-ordinated at senior management level. If the company prepares forecasts and long range plans as a normal procedure, it should be possible to assess the reliability of past forecasts.

3.77 It is important to ascertain the accounting bases employed by the company in the past in order to assess whether they are both acceptable and consistently applied in the forecast. Areas which may require particular attention include:
(a) bases for recognising profits and for providing for losses on long-term contracts;
(b) depreciation;
(c) accounting treatment of taxation;
(d) research and development of expenditure;
(e) stock and work-in-progress valuation, including treatment of obsolete, excess and slow moving items;
(f) computation of cost of sales;
(g) provision for bad debts;
(h) treatment of exceptional items;
(i) inter-group or associated company transactions.

Testing the reliability of forecasts

3.78 Where a company has adopted a system of budgeting and management accounting over a period of years, a comparison should be made between the budgets, management accounts and financial accounts for at least the last two financial years. The purpose of this is to establish the amount of care with which budgets are prepared, and the investigation and action within the company which follows variations from budget. Material variances between the budgeted and actual results as disclosed in the management accounts should be investigated, and an opinion formed of the overall reliability of the system of forecasting. The reporting accountants should also consider whether the budgets are intended to be targets or genuinely achievable estimates. A reconciliation should be prepared between the results disclosed in the management accounts and those disclosed in the financial accounts for these periods. The objective of this comparison is to show whether the management accounts have been prepared on a basis comparable with the financial accounts and to enable them to reach a conclusion concerning their general accuracy. If the conclusion drawn is that the previous history of budgeting and management accounts shows that the system is not reliable, they should proceed on the basis that the company has no history of budgeting.

3.79 In cases where the company does not have past experience of budgeting, the reporting accountants are deprived of one of their main review techniques. In such cases the method of examination of the forecast is to tabulate and review critically the previous three year's audited accounts (and management accounts, if any) for the purpose of establishing any trends which may be apparent in the results of the company's commercial operations and any recurrent accounting problems. The most recent accounts of the company should be examined, in conjunction with the audit working papers, and areas where possible difficulties may be experienced should be recognised. Using this information as a background, they should then consider carefully the procedures and bases which have been adopted in arriving at the forecast. The limiting factors affecting the forecast should be established and the forecast should be examined critically section by section. An aide-memoire is set out in Practical Guide 3.4 indicating in broad terms the factors to be borne in mind when carrying out this work. If the information available is so scanty that they may not be able to express an opinion about the forecast, the client and any other parties involved should be informed at an early stage.

Detailed examination of forecasts

3.80 The amount of detailed work done on the forecast depends largely on the results of the preliminary review and of the examination of the forecasting system. The reporting accountants should take account of all events which could affect the business and the validity of the forecast up to the date of their report thereon. The scope and time budget should be agreed in advance.

Results achieved to date

3.81 When part of an accounting period covered by a profit forecast has been completed, the results achieved to date should be tabulated and compared with the budget for that period and also with the budget and actual results for the corresponding period in the previous year. From these tabulations it should be apparent whether the company is trading in accordance with its forecast and whether seasonal variations etc show a consistent trend. Consideration should be given to the quality of interim management accounts to decide whether or not they have been prepared to a standard suitable for publication as defined above. The final decision whether the results should be disclosed in the offer document, together with comparative figures for the previous period, rests entirely with the company's board of directors, but guidance may well be requested.

Working capital forecasts

3.82 The object of the review of working capital forecasts is to satisfy the reporting accountants that the company appears to have, or to have access to, sufficient working capital to cover its trading activities and other commitments throughout a period of at least a year ahead. Where the company is operating close to its overdraft or other financial limits, forecasts should be on a monthly or at least a quarterly basis. The review should have regard to the trading levels envisaged by the profit forecast, and to other known cash commitments, eg tax payments, capital expenditure programmes and dividend payments. The forecast should be updated as near as possible to the time of the review and should be linked to current bank balances. Direct confirmation of these balances should be obtained from the company's bankers. In addition, written confirmation should be obtained from the company's bankers that overdraft or loan facilities have been granted in the amounts required and for the period covered by the working capital forecast.

DOCUMENTATION

3.83 As a general rule, copies of schedules and statistics produced by the company should be obtained where possible. Much relevant information will be obtained orally and this should always be committed to writing together with notes of work done to corroborate the statements received. At the end of fieldwork, the person responsible for the review or a section of the review should produce a statement of the outcome of any contentious matters considered during the review. An aide-memoire of the subjects to be covered by this schedule are set out in Practical Guide **3.5** together with a number of standard schedules which should be used where appropriate.

REPORTING

Published short-form reports

3.84 Reporting on an engagement of this nature is a matter of great sensitivity. Thus the reporting accountants should always consult with the company before any short-form report on a profit forecast review, which is intended for publication, is agreed. Provided that there are no material reservations about the accounting policies and the calculations for the forecast, and there are no reasons to think that they are inconsistent with the stated assumptions, the short-form report set out in Practical Guide **3.6** (Example 1) will be used.

3.85 If it is also necessary, because of the requirements of the City Code, to report on interim unaudited accounts published during the offer period, the second example set out in Practical Guide **3.6** will be used.

3.86 If it is not possible to obtain all the information required, or if there are serious reservations about the amounts, or the assumptions, or the descriptions of the forecast, or about its method of preparation, the facts, and their effect on any opinion, should be set out.

Published financial advisers' reports

3.87 Provided that the financial advisers are satisfied that the forecasts have been prepared by the directors with scrupulous care and objectivity, and that the assumptions on which the forecasts are based are meaningful and realistic, their short-form report for publication will normally be similar to the following format:

> 'We refer to the profit forecast of your company and its subsidiaries for the year ending .... 19 .. set out in .... dated .... 19 ..

92 *Profit forecasts*

addressed to yourselves from ...., the reporting accountants, regarding the accounting policies and the calculations underlying the forecast. On the basis of the assumptions made by you, the accounting policies and the calculations reviewed by ...., we consider that the profit forecast for the year ending .... 19 .., for which you are solely responsible, has been prepared with due care and consideration'.

3.88 If it is also necessary, because of the requirements of the City Code, for the financial advisers to report on interim unaudited accounts published during the offer period, the following form of combined wording may be suitable:

'With reference to the .... to be dated .... 19 .. addressed to the shareholders of ABC plc, which included the unaudited interim report of ABC plc for the six months ended .... 19 .., we have discussed with directors of your company and with ...., the reporting accountants, the bases and the assumptions upon which the unaudited interim report and the forecast have been made.

'We have also considered the letter addressed to yourselves from ...., the reporting accountants, regarding the accounting policies upon which the unaudited interim report has been prepared, and the accounting policies and the calculations upon which the forecast has been made.

'On the basis of the accounting policies and the calculations reviewed by ...., and, in the case of the profit forecast, the assumption made by the sufficiency of working capital has been made by the directors after due and careful enquiry. The issuing house usually requests either a long form report (see below) or a "letter of comfort" from the reporting accountants on this matter. If a letter of comfort is required, it would usually follow the form of Example 3 in Practical Guide **3.6**'.

Consent to publish

3.91 The reporting accountants and the financial advisers both have to give their consent to the issue of the document with the inclusion therein of their respective reports in the form and the context in which those reports appear. The letter of consent must therefore refer to the form and the context in which the report is included, and it will usually be in the following form:

'We hereby consent to the issue to the shareholders of ABC plc of the (circular) (offer by yourselves on behalf of) dated .... 19 .. with the inclusion therein of our report dated .... 19 .. in the form and the context in which it is included. A copy of the circular which has been initialled by us for identification is attached.'

The consent will be addressed to the people who are issuing the document, who may be either the directors or the financial advisers. This emphasises the need for the reporting accountants to satisfy themselves that the presentation of the forecast and other matters contained in the document are fair and reasonable, and also to satisfy themselves that no information necessary for the shareholders to reach an informed opinion has been omitted.

Consent to the extended use of forecasts

3.92 If the directors wish to make use of the same forecast and reports in a later document, they may do so only if they obtain the written consents of the reporting accountants and the financial advisers to the extended use of their reports. The reporting accountants should ensure that the directors are satisfied that the forecast is still valid and that they have included a statement to that effect in the document. The reporting accountants should also review any further information (such as management accounts drawn up to a later date) that may have become available and question the company's directors to see whether they are aware of any happenings that cast doubt on the validity of the forecast and the assumptions on which it was based. Assuming that they were so satisfied, they would give their consent in the following form:

'We hereby consent to the issue of the ....
dated .... 19 .. to ....
with the reference therein to our name and the extended use of our letter to you dated .... 19 .. (which was included in the circular of the same date sent to ....
.....) in the form and context in which such reference is included'.

Unpublished long-form reports

3.93 It is now common practice for either the financial advisers or the directors to ask reporting accountants to prepare a long-form report on the company's preparation of the profit forecast. The reporting accountants should produce their report in draft form so that it may be discussed with the financial advisers and the company's directors to ensure that there is no disagreement as to the facts or the interpretation of them. Although any possible variations to the forecast that arise from their review may be summarised, adjustment of the directors' forecast should be avoided unless such variations are specifically agreed with the directors. In preparing a long-form report, the guidelines set out in Practical Guide **3.7** should be followed.

3.94 Where the final amount of the forecast is kept open until as late a date as possible the reporting accountants may wish to finalise their long-form report on the date on which it is discussed both with the financial advisers and the directors. If the directors subsequently decide to publish the forecast, or if they vary the forecast, or if further relevant information comes to light, a supplementary report to the date on which the forcast is published would be issued.

3.1 City Code on take-overs and mergers: Practice Note No 6

RULE 16(2): PROFIT FORECASTS

Many aspects of this Rule are not capable of amplification except on an ad hoc basis, but this Note attempts to clarify such aspects as can usefully be the subject of general comment.

1   Forecasts must be prepared with scrupulous care and objectivity. It is the duty of the financial advisers to satisfy themselves that they have been prepared in this manner by the directors. In the past it has not been uncommon for the assumptions underlying a forecast to be unhelpful and uninformative; the directors should strive to make them as meaningful as possible and others concerned, namely the financial advisers and auditors or consultant accountants, should assist the directors in achieving this objective.

Forecasting profits is a hazardous exercise; in no sense is it an absolute science. The Code is designed to strike a balance so that, although there is no room for recklessness and irresponsibility, the directors do not feel inhibited from communicating to shareholders information which may be relevant to the value of their shares. Shareholders should, however, recognise that in the final analysis a forecast amounts only to an attempt to predict the future.

2   Dividend forecasts are not normally of themselves considered to be profit forecasts for the purposes of this Rule, unless, for example, they are accompanied by an estimate as to dividend cover.

3   An estimate of profits for a period which has already expired should be treated as a profit forecast within this Rule. Except with the consent of the Panel, any unaudited profits figure published during an offer period should be reported on in accordance with this Rule.

4   Except with the consent of the Panel, any forecast which has been made before the commencement of the offer period must be repeated in the document and examined and reported on in accordance with this Rule. This provision does not, however, apply to unaudited statements of annual or interim results which have already been published.

At the outset an adviser should invariably check whether or not his client has a forecast on the record, so that the reporting procedures can be set in train with a minimum of delay.

Very occasionally representations may be made to the Panel to the effect that, because of the uncertainties involved, it is not possible for a forecast previously made to be reported on in accordance with this Rule nor for a revised forecast to be made. In these circumstances the Panel would insist on shareholders being given a full explanation as to why the requirements of the Code were not capable of being met.

5   A forecast made by an offeror offering solely cash need not be reported on.

6 If a forecast, duly reported on, is included in a document, except with the consent of the Panel, any document subsequently sent out by that company in connection with that offer must contain a statement by the directors that the forecast remains valid for the purpose of the offer, and that the financial advisers and accountants who reported on the forecast have indicated that they have no objection to their reports continuing to apply.

If a forecast is repeated in the context of a different transaction from that for which the forecast was initially reported on and the repetition is within 60 days, the Panel will accept the reproduction of the original reporting letters and confirmation in the document by the directors that they know of no reason why the original forecast should not stand, and that the financial advisers and accountants who reported on the forecast have consented to the extended use of their reports.

7 It should be appreciated that even when no particular figure is mentioned certain forms of words may constitute a profit forecast. Examples are 'profits will be somewhat higher than last year' and 'the profits of the second half-year are expected to be similar to those earned in the first half-year' (when interim figures have already been published). It is impossible to generalise but broadly whenever a form of words puts a floor under (or, in certain circumstances, a ceiling on) the likely profits of a particular period or whenever a form of words contains the data necessary to ascertain an approximate figure for future profits by an arithmetical process, the Panel takes the view that there is a profit forecast which, except to the extent that in exceptional circumstances specific dispensation has first been obtained, must be reported on in accordance with this Rule. In cases of doubt professional advisers are strongly urged to consult the Panel in advance.

8 When a profit forecast is included in a document addressed to shareholders there should be included, where possible, a forecast of turnover, profit before taxation, taxation (where the figure is significantly abnormal), minority interests and extraordinary items (where either of these amounts is material).

9 Where income from land and buildings is a material element in a forecast that part of the forecast should normally be examined and reported on by a valuer.

10 Where, after an offer document has been posted, a profit forecast is given in a press announcement any assumptions on which the forecast is based should be included in the announcement. Thereafter, there should be a minimum of delay before a circular, including letters reporting on the forecast, is sent to shareholders.

11 Statements referring to prospects for limited periods (eg the following quarter) will be regarded as falling within this Rule and subject to the same treatment as a forecast for a full year.

12 In general all the relevant provisions of this Rule and the Practice Notes apply also to profit forecasts prepared on a current cost basis of accounting. The basis of computation underlying such forecasts should be stated. Any such forecast should also be accompanied by a corresponding forecast prepared on an historical cost basis.

3.2 City Code on take-overs and mergers: Practice Note No 7

RULE 16(2): THE ASSUMPTIONS ON WHICH A PROFIT FORECAST IS BASED

Requirement to state the assumptions

1 This Practice Note, upon which the Consultative Committee of Accountancy Bodies has been consulted, reviews the types of assumptions often listed in practice as the basis for a forecast and indicates how such assumptions can be framed so as to be of maximum assistance to the reader.

2 The main object of circulars is to persuade shareholders either to accept or to reject an offer. However objective a board of directors tries to be, their forecast may be coloured by the case being advocated by them or by their advisers. In addition, whereas in a prospectus it is properly the practice to make a conservative estimate of profits, in this type of circular it may be doing a disservice to shareholders to err on the conservative side. Profit forecasts in any event are always the results of personal judgment and are liable to be affected by a number of substantial uncertainties.

3 It is important therefore that by listing the assumptions on which the forecast is based some information should be given to help shareholders in forming a view as to the reasonableness and reliability of the forecast. This should include a summary of the conclusions reached by the directors on matters which required judgment as to the likely outcome of events, and should draw the shareholders' attention to, and where possible quantify, those uncertain factors which could materially disturb the ultimate achievement of the forecast.

4 From the standpoint of the directors making the forecast and of their advisers it is also right that they should be able to explain the uncertainties and so protect themselves from subsequent unjustified criticism if the forecast is not achieved.

5 The forecast and the assumptions on which it is based are the sole responsibility of the directors. However, a duty is placed on the financial advisers to discuss the assumptions with their client and to satisfy themselves that the forecast has been made with due care and consideration. Auditors or consultant accountants should satisfy themselves that the forecasts, so far as the accounting bases and calculations are concerned, have been properly compiled on the footing of the assumptions made.

Although the accountants have no responsibility for the assumptions, they will as a result of their review be in a position to advise the company on what assumptions should be listed in the circular and the way in which they should be described. The financial advisers and accountants obviously have substantial influence on the information given in a circular about assumptions. Neither should allow an assumption to be published which appears to them to be unrealistic (or one to be omitted which appears to them to be important) without commenting on it in their reports.

Detailed considerations

6 The Code gives no guidance as to what is meant by the phrase 'assumptions, including the commercial assumptions, upon which the directors have based their profit forecasts' and as would be expected this has been interpreted in a variety of ways.

7 Some assumptions have done no more than say that in making the forecast it has been assumed that the estimates used will prove to be right, for example:

> 'Sales and profits for the year will not differ materially from those budgeted for.'

> 'There will be no increases in costs other than those anticipated and provided for.'

Every forecast involves estimates of income and of costs and must obviously be dependent on these estimates. Assumptions of the type illustrated above do not help the shareholder and are better omitted, unless they are amplified so as to make them informative, eg by going on to say that sales $x\%$ up on last year's sales have been budgeted for.

8 There are inevitable limitations in the accuracy of some forecasts and shareholders will be assisted if these can be indicated. It will normally be helpful to include a description of the general nature of the business or businesses with an indication of any major hazards in forecasting in these particular businesses. So as to show the significance of any such hazards it may also be helpful if a breakdown of forecast sales and profits before tax by diverse activities can be given with a comparison with the similar figures for recent years which may have already been published under section 17 of the Companies Act 1967.

9 The assumptions stated should not relate to the accuracy of the accounting systems. Examples have been:

> 'The book record of stock and work-in-progress will be confirmed at the end of the financial year.'

> 'The estimate of stock at 31st December, 1980 will prove substantially accurate.'

If the systems of accounting and forecasting are such that full reliance cannot be placed on them, this should be the subject of some qualification in the forecast itself (perhaps also requiring a qualification in the reports of the financial advisers and accountants). It is not satisfactory for this type of deficiency to be covered by the assumptions, although any area in the estimates that is subject to special doubt should be indicated.

10   Reference has frequently been made in assumptions to unforeseen circumstances, such as:

> 'The profits anticipated will not be unduly affected by any unforeseen factors.'
>
> 'There will be no significant unforeseen circumstances.'

It must be expected that a forecast will take account of all *foreseen* circumstances and it does not seem necessary or helpful to have a general assumption about the unforeseen. However, it is a general practice in referring to profit forecasts in a prospectus to use such a phrase and this could be incorporated in the statement about the forecast in a circular, rather than as an assumption, eg:

> 'The directors forecast that, in the absence of unforeseen circumstances, the profits before tax for the year. . . .'

11   Even the more specific type of assumption may still leave the shareholder in doubt as to its implications, for instance:

> 'No abnormal liabilities will arise under guarantees.'
>
> 'Provisions for outstanding legal claims will prove adequate.'

One might dismiss these on the grounds that the first relates to the unforeseen and the second to the adequacy of the estimating system. However, the reason for the inclusion of each of these assumptions was presumably because there was an unusual element of doubt about the liabilities under guarantees and claims. In both these examples it would have been more helpful if information could have been given about the extent or basis of the provision already made and/or about the circumstances in which unprovided liabilities might arise.

12   It may be helpful to indicate what the effect on the profit forecast would be if certain of the major assumptions were to prove to be wholly or partly invalid. For example, the effect might be shown if sales volume, selling prices, raw material costs, etc were $y\%$ above/below estimate or if full production from a new factory were delayed by z months. It may be appropriate for maximum and minimum forecast profits to be given rather than a single figure.

General rules

13   It is suggested that the following general rules should apply to the selection and drafting of assumptions:
(a)   the reader should be able to understand their implications and so helped in forming a judgment as to the reasonableness of the forecast and to the main uncertainties attaching to it;

(b) the assumptions should be, wherever possible, specific rather than general, definite rather than vague;
(c) all-embracing assumptions and those relating to the general accuracy of the estimates should be avoided;
(d) the assumptions should relate only to matters which may have a material bearing on the forecast.

There is however a need for brevity and simplicity which may restrict adherence to the foregoing in every detail. There may be occasions, particularly when the forecast relates to a period already ended, when no assumptions are required.

14   The larger and more complex the group, the more difficult it becomes to make the assumptions specific and definite, with reasonable brevity. In such instances it may be appropriate to give a division of profits and to relate the assumptions specifically to the various divisions.

Examples

15   Examples of assumptions which follow these rules are given below:
(a) 'The company's present management and accounting policies will not be changed.' (For a company being acquired.)
(b) 'Interest rates and the bases and rates of taxation, both direct and indirect, will not change materially.'
(c) 'There will be no material change in international exchange rates.'
(d) 'Percentage of time lost on building sites, due to adverse weather conditions, will be average for the time of the year.'
(e) 'Turnover for the year will be £20m on the basis that sales will continue in line with levels and trends experienced to date, adjusted for normal seasonal factors; a reduction of £2m in turnover would result in a reduction of approximately £300,000 in the profit forecast.'
(f) 'Beer sales will increase in line with the trend established in the previous year, which corresponds to the national average rate of increase.'
(g) 'An increase of about 10% in subscriptions will be achieved as a result of increases in the prices of certain journals and an increase in the number of subscribers.'
(h) 'Trading results will not be affected by industrial disputes in the company's factories or in those of its principal suppliers.'
(i) 'The current national dock strike will not last longer than six weeks.'
(j) 'The new factory at Inverness will be in full production by the end of the first quarter. A delay of three months would cause the profit forecast to be reduced by £100,000.'
(k) 'Increases in labour costs will be restricted to those recently agreed with the trades unions.'
(l) 'Increases in the level of manufacturing costs for the remainder of the year will be kept within the margin of 2% allowed for in the estimates.'
(m) 'The conversion rights attaching to all the convertible loan stock will be exercised on the next conversion date.'

3.3 Profit and working capital forecast review: specimen letter of engagement

The letter of engagement may include the following references:

1 Planning meeting

'We refer to our meeting with .... on ....
...... 19 .. when you asked us to review and report on the profit forecast of your company for the year ending .... 19 .. proposed to be included in ....'

2 Responsibilities

'We explained that we would not in any way accept responsibility for the ultimate accuracy and realisation of the forecast, and that our work on the accounts for the year ending .... 19 .. would not constitute an audit.'

3 Discussions with directors and staff

'You understand that in order for us to carry out a review we should need to question directors and senior management regarding the preparation of the forecast, and you agreed that all such personnel would be available.'

4 Directors' responsibility

'The directors will take full responsibility for the forecast, and will ensure that the forecast is properly prepared and updated as necessary so that it represents their best estimate of the results they believe can be achieved. The directors also agreed to adopt the forecast formally by resolution of the full board before we report formally on it.'

5 Reporting accountants' responsibility

'We undertake to review the forecast so far as the accounting bases and calculations are concerned, and to report whether it has been properly compiled on the basis of the assumptions made by the board, and has been presented on a footing consistent with the accounting policies normally adopted by the company. We shall review the contents of any document in which you propose to publish our report before giving our consent to the document being issued with our report therein in the form and the context in which our report appears.'

6 Restriction on the scope of the reporting

'As agreed, in carrying out our review we shall not review your projections of ...., and will qualify our report accordingly.'

7 Other financial advisers

'We shall provide you and your financial advisers with a report on the preparation of the forecast and the explanations given to us.'

8 Fees

'Our fees are computed at our scale rates applicable for this type of work on the basis of the time necessarily occupied by our partners and staff of different seniority depending on the degree of responsibility and skill involved with the work.'

3.4 Profit and working capital forecast review: aide-memoire

This aide-memoire consists of a list of pertinent questions relating to the review of profit and working capital forecasts as a guide to the approach to be adopted when carrying out such a review. It is not necessarily a comprehensive list of all the matters to be considered or work to be done.

COMPANY'S METHOD OF PREPARATION

1 Is forecasting or long range planning a normal procedure carried out by the company? If so, obtain information about the company's normal procedures.

2 Does the present exercise differ from the company's normal forecasting or long range planning?

3 Have the bases and reasoning used in the preparation of the forecast been set down in writing and properly considered by the client?

4 Does the forecast cover cash flow as well as profits?

5 What methods of sales forecasting are used?

6 Has each functional section (eg sales, production costs) been prepared by or under the guidance of the executive in charge of that department?

7 Was any senior executive not involved in the preparation of the forecast? If so, consider whether this has introduced any serious weaknesses into the preparation procedures.

8 Was there adequate consultation between senior executives to co-ordinate the forecasts for sales and production?

9 Has the board of directors formally approved the forecast? If so, take copies of the minutes concerned.

10 If the company has no history of forecasting, extend our review of the forecast itself.

TESTING THE RELIABILITY OF PREVIOUS FORECASTS BUDGETS AND MANAGEMENT ACCOUNTS

1 Obtain copies of previous budgets and forecasts and of the actual results which compare with them. Obtain reconciliations between the budgets and actual results for the current year and at least the two previous years. How reliable have previous budgets and forecasts been?

2 Are budgets updated during the course of the financial year? Have substantial revisions been made in the past?

3 Based on previous experience is it likely that the forecast will be exceeded or fall short? Is it merely a target?

4 Have all material variances between budget and actual for the current year and at least the two previous years been satisfactorily explained?

5 Do variances which have arisen indicate any basic weaknesses in the procedures used in preparing either budgets or management accounts?

6 Have the management accounts of previous periods been reconciled with the final audited accounts? Do these reconciliations indicate that comparable accounting bases are being used?

7 If forecasting is not a normal practice of the company, consider what alternative methods are available to check the reliability of the forecast and the judgement of the staff preparing them.

DETAILED EXAMINATION OF FORECAST

General

1 Have realistic estimates been made concerning the activities of competitors?

2 Has a rate of inflation been assumed?

3 Are statistics available to indicate the existing share of the market of each main product or group?

4 Has information been obtained from external sources to indicate the rate of growth in the sales of each main product group? (Market surveys etc.)

5 How is any increased market share to be achieved?

6 To what extent are changes in sales prices taken into account in the sales forecasts?

7 Has provision been made for price changes in raw materials, labour rates and other costs?

8 To what extent has information been obtained from outside sources concerning future trends of prices of major raw materials?

9 What are the reasons for any predicted major changes in the percentages of costs to sales? Has this been explained for each product?

10   Has the effect on unit costs resulting from predicted major changes in production volumes been reflected in the forecasts?

11   Has the effect of any possible change in sales mix on the forecast profitability been examined?

12   To what extent are sales or supplies of materials dependent on long term contracts and, if significant, are they at fixed prices?

13   Has appropriate consideration been given to any acquisition or disposal of major assets or business which may occur?

14   Has the likelihood of achievement of the sales and production forecasts been examined in relation to any major capital projects which might not be completed on time?

15   Are the necessary raw materials and labour force readily available to meet the forecast requirements?

16   Has consideration been given to the effect on overhead expenses of inflation, capital expenditure, changes in sales patterns, production methods, etc?

17   Is the previous pattern in trading with other companies in the group and/or associated companies likely to continue?

Favourable and unfavourable factors taken into account

18   To what extent does the forecast depend on the success of new and untried products or markets? Are any previously successful products now vulnerable from obsolescence or new competition?

19   Have products making losses or breaking even been considered as carefully as those making the major contribution to the company's profits?

20   Has provision been made for possible government restriction (eg price increases, credit/hire controls, purchase tax)?

21   Are forecasts influenced or likely to be influenced by present export tariff agreements regarding both exports and imports? Have possible changes in tariffs been taken into account?

Consistent accounting bases

22   Have there been any changes in accounting methods or bases during the previous years under consideration which materially affect the apparent sales or profits trend?

23   Have proper adjustments been made for intergroup/division transactions and unrealised profits?

24 Have intergroup/division transactions been accounted for on an appropriate and consistent basis?

Contingencies

25 What margin for contingencies has been included in the forecast and where?

Arithmetical accuracy

26 Has the arithmetical accuracy of the forecast been checked?

27 Have interdivision/intercompany accounts been agreed?

RESULTS ACHIEVED TO DATE

1 Has consideration been given to all material variations between the actual, forecast and prior year's figures in relation to the latest management accounts and their possible effect on the forecast for the remainder of the period?

2 Where the company's trade is subject to seasonal fluctuations do the latest results show a consistent trend?

3 Have there been any material adjustments subsequent to the approval of the profit forecast?

4 Have there been any major events subsequent to the approval of the profit forecast which might affect its validity?

5 Are there interim accounts in a state and form suitable for publication (ie are they up to the standard of published but unaudited or preliminary final accounts)?

WORKING CAPITAL FORECAST

1 When was the working capital forecast (i) prepared (ii) formally approved?

2 Has it been updated in preparation for the current review?

3 Has it recognised:
(a) Profit forecast results?
(b) Capital expenditure budgets?
(c) Other financial commitments (eg taxation and dividend)?

4 Are the credit periods, for receipt of cash from debtors and for payments to creditors, which have been assumed in the forecast, reasonable?

5 Did the working capital forecast commence from agreed and certified bank reconciliations?

6 If overdraft or loan facilities are required during the period have these been agreed by the proposed lenders in writing to the company and independently confirmed by you?

3.5 Profit and working capital forecast review: specimen working papers

The specimens set out in this Practical Guide are intended to illustrate the content of certain standard schedules which should appear on every review file.

1 Typical contents of salient features schedule.

2 Previous year: comparison of actual and budgeted results.

3 Current year: comparison of budgets and actual results for completed period.

SPECIMEN 1: TYPICAL CONTENTS OF SALIENT FEATURES SCHEDULE

The schedule of salient features should be prepared by the assistant manager, supervisor or senior in charge of field work and should contain conclusions on the salient features of the forecast and in particular observations, on the following questions:

1 Do you conclude that the people who prepared the forecasts have been realistic in their assessment and have good grounds for the assumptions and bases used in preparation of the forecast?

2 Are their judgments proven by past experience and if not, are you satisfied that you have used a sound basis to assess them?

3 What are the essential assumptions which, in your opinion, must hold good if the forecast is to be achieved?

4 What comments have you as to the likelihood of these assumptions holding good?

5 If any of your comments cast doubt on the likelihood of some assumptions holding good, what provision has been made for this in the forecast?

6 What unbudgeted events might reasonably happen and what would be the effect on the forecast result (eg strikes, devaluation, changes in interest rates, failure of a source of supply etc)?

7 What margins for contingencies are included in the forecast or what margins do you consider appropriate?

8 Has the aggregation of the different sections of the forecast been considered as a whole? Are you sure that the forecast has been reviewed in its proper perspective?

9 Have the calculations been checked and double checked? Have the implications of adjustments to any part of the forecast on other parts of the forecast been properly taken into account?

10 As a result of your review, do you conclude that the accounting bases and calculations of the forecasts are acceptable? What are your reasons?

Profit and working capital forecast review: specimen working papers 111

Client: Specimen 2
Subject: Previous Year Comparison of Actual and Budgeted Results
Year end:

Prepared by
Date:

Reviewed by
Date:

Schedule

					Current Year Forecast	Previous Year	
						Budget	Actual

112 *Profit and working capital forecast review: specimen working papers*

Client: Specimen 3

Subject: Current Year — Comparison of Budgets and Actual Results for Completed Period

Prepared by:
Date:

Reviewed by:
Date:

Schedule

Year end:

						Current period x months to xxx 19xx		Previous period x months to xxx 19xx	
						Budget	Actual	Budget	Actual

3.6 Profit and working capital forecast review: specimen short-form reports

EXAMPLE 1

Short-form report on directors' profit forecast

(For use where there are no material reservations about the accounting policies and the calculations for the forecast, and there are no reasons to think that they are inconsistent with the stated assumptions.)

> 'We have reviewed the accounting bases and the calculations for the profit forecast of ABC plc and its subsidiaries, for which you as directors are solely responsible, for the year ending 31 December 19.., set out in the offer document dated .... 19.., addressed to .... The profit forecast is based on the latest information available including (unaudited management accounts/audited interim accounts for the .... months ended .... 19..).
>
> In our opinion, the profit forecast so far as the accounting bases and calculations are concerned, has been properly compiled on the footing of the assumptions made by you and set out in the offer document, and is presented on a basis consistent with the accounting policies normally adopted by ABC plc and its subsidiaries.'

EXAMPLE 2

Short-form report on directors' profit forecast

(Addendum for use where it is necessary, because of the requirements of the City Code, to report on interim unaudited accounts published during the offer period.)

> 'We have reviewed the compilation of the statement of unaudited results of ABC plc for the six months ended .... 19.. included in the document dated .... 19.. addressed to the company's shareholders. Such a review is substantially less in scope than an examination made in accordance with approved auditing standards, and it would not necessarily disclose all relevant matters of significance.
>
> Within the limitatiaons of our review, we have formed the opinion that the unaudited results, for which the directors are solely responsible, have been properly compiled by them on the basis of accounting practices normally adopted by the company.'

EXAMPLE 3

Short-form report of directors' profit forecast

(Form of 'letter of comfort' to issuing house).

'We have considered the opinion expressed by the directors of the company that, taking into account the bank facilities available, the company and its subsidiaries have sufficient working capital to meet their present requirements.

On the basis of information and explanations made available to us by the directors and of the forecast of profits (for which the directors are solely responsible) on the basis of the assumption made for the year ending .... 19 .., we are of the opinion that the company and its subsidiaries have sufficient working capital to meet their present requirements.'

3.7 Profit and working capital forecast review: illustration of the contents of an unpublished long-form report

INTRODUCTION

The introduction should include the following matters as a minimum.

1 Confirmation of the client's instructions (it may be appropriate to attach the letter of engagement as an appendix).

2 Scope of work undertaken.

3 Any restrictions the company has placed on the scope of the reporting accountants' examination.

4 State the audience for which the report is intended in the following words:

> 'This report is intended solely for the information of ....
> .... for the purposes of .... It should not otherwise be used, quoted or circulated for any other purpose without our permission.'

5 A reference to the respective responsibilities of the directors and the reporting accountants.

6 The state of the basic accounting records (ie are they up to date?).

COMPOSITION OF THE FORECAST

1 Specify the periods covered by the audited accounts, the unaudited management accounts and the projected figures.

2 Refer to the dates on which the company's officials and directors prepared, revised and approved the forecast, (if possible there should be specific reference to the relevant board minute) and also to the dates of the reporting accountants' examination.

3 Specify the reporting subsidiaries, units or divisions that are included in the group forecast, and indicate the way in which each is dealt with in the report.

CONCLUSIONS

1 Summarise the areas in which the forecast appears to be either unduly optimistic or unduly pessimistic.

2 Comment on the amount of any contingency margin relative to the above.

3 Set out, in full, the wording, including the assumptions, to be used in any document by the directors.

4 List any matters which (in the opinion of the reporting accountants) should be minuted by the directors when they approve the forecasts and the above wording for inclusion in the document.

5 If appropriate, express an opinion using as a basis the specimen short-form report.

THE PROFIT FORECAST

1 Set out the group forecast figures as a pro-forma profit and loss account.

2 Analyse each of the above figures (namely audited, unaudited, and forecast).

3 Give comparative figures for equivalent periods in the preceding year (if these are available).

4 Tabulate the contribution to earnings of each of the principal subsidiaries or divisions.

COMPILATION OF THE FORECAST

1 Describe the method by which the group normally prepares, reviews and revises the integral parts of a forecast for subsidiaries, units or divisions of the group.

2 Describe any additional reviews or revisions carried out for the forecast under review.

3 Name and describe the responsibilities of the company's senior management who were responsible for the various procedures involved in preparing and reviewing the forecast.

HISTORY OF FORECASTING

1 Describe the group's experience of forecasting.

2 Compare the previous years' forecasts with the final audited results.

3 Explain the principal differences indentified by that comparison.

ASSUMPTIONS

1 List the principal assumptions on which the group forecast is based and which the directors intend to publish.

2 Refer to any assumptions that are recited in the forecasts of the divisions, but which the directors do not intend to list with the principal assumptions.

3 Include a sensitivity analysis, quantifying, where possible, the effect that any particular assumption will have on the forecast results if it proves to be wrong.

ACCOUNTING POLICIES

1 State whether the accounting policies used are those normally adopted by the group in its published accounts.

2 Explain any variations used in preparing the forecast.

3 Specify the exchange rates used for the purpose of the forecast.

4 State how the exchange rates have been applied and how exchange differences have been treated.

SUBSIDIARIES AND DIVISIONS

1 Summarise the forecast for each reporting division. Analyse the forecast between audited, unaudited and forecast figures, and give comparisons for equivalent periods in the preceding year.

2 Include (as an appendix) pro-forma manufacturing, trading and detailed profit and loss accounts (where these are sufficiently material in the context of the group as a whole).

3 Comment on the comparisons of the forecast with audited figures of the previous year.

4 Name and describe the responsibilities of the managers of the subsidiary or division who were responsible for preparing the forecast, or for the relevant parts of it, and with whom it has been discussed. Refer to explanations those managers gave of all significant variations.

5 List the principal assumptions used, and include a sensitivity analysis quantifying, where possible, the effect that any particular assumption will have on the forecast results if it proves to be wrong.

6 Comment (as necessary) on taxation and extraordinary items.

7 If appropriate, indicate where the forecast may prove to be either too optimistic or too pessimistic.

HEAD OFFICE

1 Include similar information to that for each reporting division.

2 Comment on the reconciliation of inter-company accounts and the inclusion in the forecast of inter-company charges or credits.

3 Describe all matters dealt with centrally (such as pension fund deficiencies, legal actions, the discontinuance of operations, etc) and all normal consolidation adjustments and eliminations.

4 Detail any errors found in the calculations, and particularly refer to any items that may prove either too optimistic or too pessimistic.

WORKING CAPITAL FORECAST

1 Describe how the cash flow projections were prepared.

2 Summarise the cash flow projections over the period of the forecast. Describe the cash resources available and draw attention to any resources that may need to be renegotiated.

3 Identify any additional assumptions made in preparing the cash flow projection.

TAXATION

Comment on the compilation of the forecast taxation charge, and give explanations as to why the overall rate differs from the standard rate of tax applicable.

EXTRAORDINARY ITEMS

Give details of any known or expected extraordinary items, and comment on any matters that may have to be treated as extraordinary in the next published accounts. In addition, give details and explanations of any last-minute revisions made to the group forecast.

3.8 Profit and working capital forecasts: forecasting working papers

The purpose of the schedules set out in this Practical Guide is to provide outlines of working papers which may be useful in preparing forecasts. It is not possible to take into account all factors which may be important in any one business and it will be necessary to adapt the suggested layouts to the particular requirements of the business concerned.

It is assumed in these schedules that the forecast period is for the next twelve months. Taxation (corporation tax and advance corporation tax) has been ignored other than providing for its payment in the cash forecast. It has also been assumed that all credit purchases are of stocks.

PROFIT FORECAST

The forecasting schedules are based on the forecast of profits for the forecast period. In general, this will be made up from three forecasts:

1   Sales forecast.
2   Production cost and gross margin forecast.
3   Overheads forecast.

SALES FORECAST

This is likely to be the most important element of the profit forecast. In most businesses it will be necessary to phase the sales forecast by each month in accordance with past trading experience, rather than just spread an annual forecast equally over each month.

It will be necessary to forecast the expected volume or sales as well as their value. In preparing its forecast of sales, a business should at least consider the following matters:

(a)   What will be the effect of national economic conditions?
(b)   What is the extent of the order book? What degree of confidence can be placed on obtaining anticipated orders?
(c)   What is the current sales experience?
(d)   What is the trend of sales?
(e)   What monthly incidence of sales is expected, and what is past experience?
(f)   What will be the effect of competition?
(g)   What is the outlook for the market?
(h)   Are there capacity constraints on the sales forecast (eg production, distribution or administration)?
(i)   What effect of marketing policy is forecast?
(j)   What is the outlook for large customers?
(k)   Are forecast discounts realistic?

(l) Are forecast margins realistic?
(m) What is the forecast effect of price rises by the business on volume and margins?
(n) Is the sales manager committed to the forecast?
(o) Are other relevant managers (eg production) committed?

Once these matters have been considered and a forecast calculated, the forecast sales should be entered on Schedule 1 distinguishing between cash and credit sales.

PRODUCTION COSTS AND GROSS MARGIN FORECAST

The second element of the profit forecast is the forecast of gross margins resulting from the expected volume and value of sales. This in turn is affected by forecasts of the cost of materials, labour and factory overheads. In producing these forecasts, a business should at least consider the following matters:

(a) Is production capacity sufficient to meet the sales forecast? Is more machinery or space required?
(b) How do forecast margins differ from past results?
(c) Are raw material costs forecast to rise; when?
(d) Can increased raw material costs and labour costs be passed on?
(e) Are any cost escalation clauses adequate to maintain margins?
(f) Are raw materials supplies readily available?
(g) What is the basis of forecast wage increases in the period. What will be the effect?
(h) Is labour at the rates envisaged readily available?
(i) Has stock wastage and obsolescence been taken into account?
(j) What are the costs of increased production? (consider whether bonuses must be paid, new manpower recruited or new machinery purchased).
(k) Is existing machinery reliable?
(l) Is there sufficient storage space?
(m) Are productivity increases forecast, and on what basis?
(n) What is the effect of a change in the sales mix on overall margins?

When the necessary calculations have been completed, the forecasts of direct costs can be entered in Schedule 1.

OVERHEAD FORECAST

The overhead forecast shows the overhead costs which must be incurred in order to achieve the forecast level of sales.

Overheads are usually best forecast on a line by line basis, in conjunction with those managers concerned. Inflation and the underlying level of overheads should be taken into account, and help can be obtained in forecasting individual items by (for example) obtaining information from suppliers and/or the manager responsible, or by increasing overheads at the forecast inflation rate.

The forecast should be consistent with the sales/production forecast; for example many overhead items (commissions, postage, transport, phones), will rise with an increased volume of sales.

The total detailed overheads shown in Schedule 2 can then be summarised in Schedule 1.

OTHER MATTERS

Breakeven level of sales

It is useful to forecast the breakeven level of sales, which can be calculated by dividing forecast overheads by the forecast gross margin percentage. This shows the level of sales at which forecast gross margins are equal to the forecast level of overheads. In the forecast period some costs which are traditionally regarded as variable, such as production wages, may in the time scale involved more properly be regarded as fixed and should be treated as overheads. The schedules are not drafted to highlight these distinctions and it may in particular cases be useful to redraft them to show this.

Finance costs

These can only be accurately forecast after the cash forecast has been prepared.

Assumptions and other statements

These can be appended to Schedule 1 or shown separately.

Capital expenditure forecast

This is required both for the cash forecast and for the forecast of the depreciation change.

CASH FLOW FORECAST

The purpose of a cash flow forecast is to show the cash effects of the profit forecast.
　The assumptions underlying the cash forecast are as important as those underlying the profit forecast.
　A systematic approach should be adopted in the same way as for the profit forecast.
　If financial facilities cannot be negotiated to meet any shortfall between the bank and other financial facilities available and the forecast facilities required, then it is necessary either to amend the business plan on which the original profit forecast was based in order to allow the business to trade within its financial constraints, or to negotiate the necessary facilities.
　It will be easiest to produce the cash forecast and the subsequent balance sheet forecast (if this is required) if a fully balanced set of accounts is available for the start of the forecasting period.

Profit and working capital forecasts: forecasting working papers

Cash receipts

Cash receipts from credit sales in any one month should be entered in the months in which their receipt is expected, and an example of a schedule which may be used to do this is shown in Schedule 4. The totals of cash receipts in each month from credit sales can then be summarised in the cash forecast (Schedule 3).

Receipts from cash sales can be entered directly on Schedule 3 from the sales forecast (Schedule 1).

If the balance sheet is to be forecast, the relevant figures should also be entered in Schedule 5.

Cash payments

(a) *Credit purchases of raw materials.* These should be spread in the same way as for credit sales, taking into account the fact that purchases shown in the profit forecast will generally not be paid for in the month of purchase. The working paper to be used is shown in Schedule 4, and the total of cash payments in each months can then be summarised in the cash forecast (Schedule 3). If the balance sheet is to be forecast, the relevant figures should be entered in Schedule 5.

(b) *Overheads.* If overheads on a cash basis do not differ significantly from those forecast on a profits basis (Schedules 1 and 2) no adjustment on to a cash basis will be necessary, and overheads on a cash basis can be entered directly in Schedule 3.

If, however, periodic payments are a significant part of forecast overheads, the cash effect of their timing should be taken into account. A working paper which may be useful is shown in Schedule 4. An alternative method to forecasting overheads on a cash basis is to forecast these independently of the profit forecast by entering them directly on to a Schedule such as Schedule 2 (retitled 'Overhead cash forecast') rather than by adjusting the 'Overhead profit forecast' as envisaged in Schedule 4.

Depreciation is deducted from overheads shown in the profit forecast since it is an item which is not expended in cash.

Other matters

(a) *PAYE, NHI.* It has been assumed that this is paid at the same time as net wages. The short period of credit allowed for PAYE and NHI payments may be taken into account if required.

(b) *VAT.* The timing of VAT payments is considered further below (see also Schedule 5). Only net payments to or from HM Customs and Excise should be shown separately in the cash forecast; receipts from debtors and payments to creditors will include VAT.

Completion of cash forecast

Schedule 3 is completed by entering forecast capital expenditure, loan repayments and other non-trading items.

The difference between total cash receipts and cash payments is the net cash flow in the period. The opening cash balance (whether positive or in overdraft) is adjusted by the net cash flow to arrive at the closing balance.

FORECASTING THE BALANCE SHEET

Once the profit and cash forecast have been prepared, it is a fairly simple matter to forecast the balance sheet at the close of the forecast period (and if required at the close of each month in the period). It is also useful to check on the reasonableness of the forecast balance sheet by setting out important accounting ratios. Layouts which may be of help in forecasting individual balance sheet items on a monthly basis are set out in Schedule 5 and are commented on below.

Forecasting the balance sheet will be found to be easiest if the profit and cash forecasts, and the subsidiary forecasts required for the balance sheet forecast (shown in Schedule 5) are done in their entirety and balanced off for the particular month concerned. This provides a completely self checking system which avoids arithmetical errors.

Debtors

The closing sales debtors in any month are:

Opening sales debtors	£x
Forecast credit sales in months	x
	x
Less: cash receipts in month from all credit sales	x
Closing sales debtors	£x

This is shown in Schedule 5; credit sales include VAT. In view of the importance of this to some businesses a separate forecast of net VAT receipts or payments may be required and a suggested layout for this is shown in Schedule 5.

Bad debts and cash discounts payable can, if required, be shown by incorporating separate columns in the Schedule.

Creditors

Opening purchase creditors	£x
Forecast creditor purchases in months	x
	x
Less: cash payments in months for all credit purchases	x
Closing purchase creditors	£x

This is shown in Schedule 5.
Discounts received can be shown separately on the Schedule as required.

VAT

A suggested layout for the net VAT receipt from or payment to HM Customs and Excise forecast is shown in Schedule 5.

Stock and work-in-progress

A suggested layout for forecasting this is shown in Schedule 5. Closing stock and work-in-progress in any one month is:

Opening stock and work-in-progress	£x
Stock purchases (exc VAT—cash	x
—credit	x
	x
Add: direct labour and related factory overheads	x
	x
Less: cost of sales	x
Closing stock and work-in-progress	£x

These figures will be derived from and/or feed into the profit forecast (Schedule 1); it will be necessary to produce the forecast of stock and work-in-progress in tandem with the profit forecast.

Fixed assets

Closing fixed assets will be arithmetically equal to opening fixed assets plus purchases, less disposals, and less depreciation. The fixed asset forecast therefore involves both the profit and the cash forecast.

Prepayments and accruals

These can be calculated (if significant) in a net total or separately from both the profit and cash forecasts as follows:

Opening overhead creditors/prepayments	£x
Add: Total overheads in profit forecast (Schedule 1)	x
Less: Total overheads in cash forecast (Schedule 4)	(x)
Closing overhead creditors/prepayments	£x

COMPUTER MODELLING

Financial modelling packages are now available which remove the reiterative drudgery of forecasting. Commercial forecasting services are also available.

SCHEDULE 1

X LTD
Profit Forecast £'000 for the (year) ended (31 December 19xx)

	ACTUAL		FORECAST*											
Year to 31.12.xx	19×0	19×1	19×2	Jan	Feb	Mar	Apr	May	Jun	Jul	Aug	Sept	Oct	Nov	Dec
SALES															
Cash															
Credit															
COST OF SALES															
Material—cash															
—credit															
Labour															
Factory overheads															
Stock and WIP adjustment**															
DIRECT COSTS															
GROSS PROFIT (%)															
OVERHEAD EXPENSES (Schedule 2)															
Selling & Distribution															
Administration															
Directors															
(%)															
OPERATING PROFIT (%)															
MISCELLANEOUS INCOME															
LESS EXPENSES															
Finance costs (Schedule 2)															
PROFIT BEFORE TAX															

* Forecast for year, phased by month
** Opening less closing stock and work in progress (Schedule 5)

SCHEDULE 2

X LTD
Profit Forecast £'000 for the (year) ended (31 December 19xx): Overhead Forecast

Year to 31.12.xx	ACTUAL 19×0	19×1	FORECAST* 19×2	Jan	Feb	Mar	Apr	May	Jun	Jul	Aug	Sept	Oct	Nov	Dec
FACTORY															
Factory management Salaries/NHI/Pension															
Rent & Rates															
Transport costs															
Machine maintenance & spares															
Heat & Light															
Consumables															
Obsolescence/Stock losses															
Machine depreciation															
TOTAL (As Schedule 1)															
SELLING AND DISTRIBUTION															
Salaries/NHI/Pension															
Discounts given															
Commissions															
Bad debts															
Entertainment/travel															
Printing/stationery															
Advertising/promotion															
Depreciation of motor vehicles															
TOTAL															

* Forecast for year, phased by month

ADMINISTRATION
Salaries/NHI/Pension
Rent & Rates
Insurances
Telephone & Postage
Travel
Entertaining
Audit
Professional fees
Cleaning

Depreciation of furniture
& office machinery

TOTAL

DIRECTORS
Salaries/NHI/Pensions
Travel/Entertainment

TOTAL

FINANCE COSTS
Bank interest
Loan interest
Leasing
HP

TOTAL

SCHEDULE 3

X LTD
Cash Forecast £'000 for the (year) ended (31 December 19xx)

	TOTAL	Jan	Feb	Mar	Apr	May	Jun	Jul	Aug	Sept	Oct	Nov	Dec
CASH RECEIPTS													
Sales—Cash (Schedule 1)													
—Credit (Schedule 4)													
VAT (net receipts)													
Other income													
Sales of assets													
Other receipts													
TOTAL													
CASH PAYMENTS													
Material—Credit (Schedule 4)													
—Cash (Schedule 1)													
Labour (Schedule 1)													
Overheads (Schedule 4)													
Taxation													
VAT (net payments)													
Capital expenditure													
Loan repayments													
Other													
TOTAL													
NET CASH FLOW													
BALANCE AT START													
BALANCE AT END													

SCHEDULE 4

X LTD
Working Papers for Cash Forecast £'s for the (year) ended (31 December 19xx)

CASH RECEIPTS FROM CREDIT SALES

Credit sale in:	TOTAL	Cash receipts in:											
		Jan	Feb	Mar	Apr	May	Jun	Jul	Aug	Sept	Oct	Nov	Dec
Previous year													
January													
February													
March													
April													
May													
June													
July													
August													
September													
October													
November													
December													
TOTAL													

CASH PAYMENTS FOR CREDIT PURCHASES

Credit sale in:	TOTAL	Cash payments in:											
		Jan	Feb	Mar	Apr	May	Jun	Jul	Aug	Sept	Oct	Nov	Dec
Previous year													
January													
February													
March													
April													
May													
June													
July													
August													
September													
October													
November													
December													
TOTAL													

Profit and working capital forecasts: forecasting working papers

OVERHEADS	TOTAL	Jan	Feb	Mar	Apr	May	Jun	Jul	Aug	Sept	Oct	Nov	Dec
Overheads from profit forecast (Schedule 1)													
Factory													
Selling & Distribution													
Administration													
Finance													
Directorate													
Less:													
Depreciation (from Schedule 2)													
Periodic payments:													
Rent													
Loan interest													
Leasing/HP													
etc													
Add:													
Periodic payments													
Rent													
Interest													
Leasing/HP													
etc													
OVERHEADS ON CASH BASIS													

SCHEDULE 5

X Ltd
Working Papers for Balance Sheet Forecast £'s for the (year) ended (31 December 19xx)

DEBTORS FORECAST

Month	Opening debtors	Credit sales in month			Receipts	Closing debtors
		Credit sales	VAT	Total		
January						
February						
March						
April						
May						
June						
July						
August						
September						
October						
November						
December						
TOTALS						

RAW MATERIALS CREDITORS FORECAST

Month	Opening creditors	Credit purchases in month			Payments	Closing creditors
		Purchases	VAT	Total		
January						
February						
March						
April						
May						
June						
July						
August						
September						
October						
November						
December						
TOTALS						

VAT FORECAST

Month	Opening creditor (debtor)	Inputs		Outputs		Net in month	Cash (Payment) Receipt	Closing creditor (debtor)
		Cash purchases	Credit purchases	Cash sales	Credit sales			
January								
February								
March								
April								
May								
June								
July								
August								
September								
October								
November								
December								
TOTALS								

STOCK AND WORK-IN-PROGRESS FORECAST

Month	Opening stock & WIP	Stock purchases (cash & credit)	Direct labour & production overheads	Cost of sales	Closing stock & WIP
January					
February					
March					
April					
May					
June					
July					
August					
September					
October					
November					
December					
TOTALS					

Chapter 4

Listing Particulars and Stock Exchange Circulars

INTRODUCTION	4.01
TECHNICAL REQUIREMENTS	4.02
Statutory and Stock Exchange requirements	4.10
Content of the accountant's report	4.12
Six months rule	4.15
Acquisition reports	4.16
Accountants' responsibilities and scope of examination	4.18
The subject entity	4.37
Adjustments to profits and assets	4.48
Documents required by The Stock Exchange	4.58
FIELDWORK	4.70
Planning	4.70
Evidence	4.75
REVIEW OF FINANCIAL STATEMENTS	4.80
PRACTICAL GUIDES	
Stock Exchange documents: summary of listing and other requirements	4.1
Unlisted Securities Market: requirements in respect of securities of a company seeking admission to the USM	4.2
Companies Act requirements for prospectuses	4.3
Contents of listing particulars (new listing)	4.4
Checklist—contents of an accountant's report (listed companies)	4.5
Specimen accountant's report	4.6
Variations to the specimen accountant's report	4.7
Listing particulars and Stock Exchange circulars: accountants' letters	4.8
Listing particulars and Stock Exchange circulars: specimen statement of adjustments	4.9

INTRODUCTION

4.01 This chapter is intended to provide guidance on the work the investigating accountants are required to carry out, and the report they are required to make, in connection with listing particulars, certain circulars to shareholders, prospectuses and other similar documents.

TECHNICAL REQUIREMENTS

4.02 The minimum contents for listing particulars to be issued by a company seeking a listing on The Stock Exchange are specified in The Stock Exchange (Listing) Regulations 1984, and in The Stock Exchange's *Admission of Securities to Listing* (The Stock Exchange Yellow Book) Section 3. It is essential that anyone likely to become involved in this type of engagement should be familiar with the requirements of *The Stock Exchange Yellow Book*.

4.03 The reporting accountant is also required by The Stock Exchange to produce an accountant's report in connection with certain acquisitions or disposals of assets, liabilities or investments (as defined by *The Stock Exchange Yellow Book*), and an accountant's report is required to be included in documents issued in connection with certain schemes of arrangement under CA 1985 s 425.

4.04 In all other cases where a company intends to offer any of its shares or debentures for sale to or subscription by the public and listing particulars do not apply, the prospectus requirements specified in CA 1985 ss 56, 57, 62, 66 and Sch 3 must be observed.

4.05 In any case, where an accountant's report which is not subject to *The Stock Exchange Yellow Book* is required, best practice dictates that its provisions are applied wherever possible.

4.06 Whenever listing particulars or a prospectus are being issued, a reporting accountant may be required to write a detailed report for the merchant bank, broker or other institution sponsoring the issue, which covers various aspects of the company's business, including its management, profit record, assets and liabilities and prospects. This type of report, commonly referred to as a 'long-form' report, is dealt with in Chapter 3.

4.07 Quite apart from his duty to prepare an accountant's report, the reporting accountant is required by *The Stock Exchange Yellow Book* to examine and report on the accounting policies and calculations for any profit forecast included in the prospectus. Such reports are dealt with in Chapter 3.

4.08 A summary of the situations in which *The Stock Exchange Yellow Book* may require listing particulars and circulars to be issued, together with an indication of the role which the reporting accountant would be required to fulfil, is set out in Practical Guide **4.1**.

4.09 As an alternative to listing, a company may apply to The Stock Exchange for admission to the Unlisted Securities Market ('USM'). When a company with its shares traded in the USM is proposing to raise additional share capital, or market its existing shares, a prospectus complying with the USM regulations and with CA 1985 is required, and the reporting accountant is required to produce an accountant's report. An accountant's report is not always necessary when a company is being introduced to the USM, but in practice such a report is often required by the sponsors to the introduction. The requirements with respect to documents published by USM companies are set out in Practical Guide **4.2**.

Statutory and Stock Exchange requirements

4.10 A prospectus is an invitation to the public to subscribe for, or to purchase, shares or debentures in a company. CA 1985 s 56 requires that such a prospectus must include the matters and the reports specified in Sch 3 of the 1985 Act. However, where the company making the offer is also seeking a listing on The Stock Exchange for those securities, The Stock Exchange (Listing) Regulations 1984 remove the CA 1985 prospectus requirements and instead impose the more rigorous 'listing particulars' requirements.

4.11 Both The Stock Exchange (Listing) Regulations 1984 and CA 1985 require the listing particulars prospectus to be produced by the directors of the company issuing the shares or debentures, and they must collectively and individually accept full responsibility for the completeness and accuracy of the information given in the document. The document will include a considerable amount of information on the company's financial affairs and will also include reports by 'experts', one of whom is the reporting accountant. A merchant bank, or broker, will usually be sponsoring the issue and will take the lead in organising the preparation of the prospectus and in obtaining the various reports which the prospectus is required to contain.

Content of the accountant's report

4.12 The purpose of the accountant's report is to provide prospective investors with such financial information as will assist them in deciding whether to invest in the company. The basic content of prospectuses is prescribed by CA 1985 Sch 3 (see Practical Guide **4.3**) and where listing particulars are required, by the more stringent Rules and Regulations of The Stock Exchange. The requirements of The Stock Exchange in respect of other circulars are less stringent. *The Stock Exchange Yellow Book* requirements in respect of listing particulars are set out in Practical Guide **4.4** and in respect of circulars in Practical Guide **4.5** A summary of *The Stock Exchange Yellow Book* requirements for accountants' reports is set out in Practical Guide **4.6** and an example of such a report is set out in Practical Guide **4.7**. However, the basic requirements in respect of accountants' reports are the following in respect of each of the five completed financial years preceding publication of the listing particulars or circular, or in respect of each of the financial years since incorporation of the company or (where

relevant) the commencement of the business if this occurred less than five years prior to publication:
(a) profits or losses of the company (or group);
(b) balance sheets of the company (or group);
(c) source and application of funds statements;
(d) earnings and dividend per share; and;
(e) various other items, including any matters which appear to be relevant for the purposes of the report.

4.13 In making the report, the reporting accountants are to make such adjustments as they consider necessary. A statement of these adjustments reconciling the figures in the report with the corresponding figures in the audited accounts must be submitted to The Stock Exchange at least 14 days before publication.

4.14 The accounting policies followed in dealing with items which are judged material or critical in determining the profits and net assets and any significant departure from standards of accounting practice must be disclosed and the latter explained. Statements of recommended practice issued by the UK accountancy bodies are also expected to be observed (Adjustments to comply with UK standards of accounting practice are not required to be made to reports relating to foreign companies applying for UK listing, but a clear statement of the accounting policies should be given. It is expected, however, that these policies will comply with the IASC International Accounting Standards).

Six months rule

4.15 The figures reported on must not be more than six months old at the date of publication of the listing particulars, and if the period covered by the report ended on a date more than three months before such publication, the report must state that no accounts have been prepared for distribution to members since that date.

Acquisition reports

4.16 A similar report is required to be given by qualified accountants who are named in the document with respect to a business or controlling interest in an unlisted company which has been acquired by the company or any of its subsidiaries since the last accounting date, or which is to be acquired.

4.17 In making such report the accountants shall make such adjustments (if any) as they consider appropriate.

Accountants' responsibilities and scope of examination

Direct responsibility

4.18 CA 1985 ss 67–70 impose civil and criminal liabilities on directors, promoters and experts with respect to prospectuses containing untrue statements. Section 71 states that a statement included in a prospectus shall be deemed to be untrue if it is misleading in the form and context in which it is included. In the case of listing particulars, however, these sections are disapplied by The Stock Exchange (Listing) Regulations 1984, which instead impose a similar liability on the persons responsible for the listing particulars only (usually the directors).

4.19 In any event, though the reporting accountant has a direct responsibility to those to whom his report is addressed. The issuing house and the company, for instance, have recourse against the accountant if they suffer damages as a result of acting upon his report, if this contained false or misleading information which materially affected the decision of the reader.

Opinion

4.20 Although the Companies Acts impose no specific opinion requirement for accountants' reports in prospectuses, *The Stock Exchange Yellow Book* requires that the accountants' report in listing particulars or a circular should express an opinion whether, for the purpose of the listing particulars or circular, a true and fair view is given of the state of affairs at the end of the period, and of the profits or losses and source and application of funds of the periods covered by the report (*The Stock Exchange Yellow Book* Section 4 para 7).

Reporting accountants who are not the company's auditors

4.21 In the case of a prospectus the company's auditor is statutorily required to act as reporting accountant, or to participate with others in that function. However in listing particulars or in a report on an acquisition any accountant who is 'independent' to the same degree as is required of the company's auditors may make the report.

4.22 A reporting accountant who is a signatory to an accountants' report will, whether he is the company's auditor or not, be expressing his own opinion as to the truth and fairness of the view shown by the financial information presented in the report.

4.23 Consequently, the reporting accountant must carry out an examination sufficient to sustain the opinion he gives. This examination will not normally be so extensive for each of the years under review as would be required for an audit of the accounts for each separate year. As well as having the considerable benefit of hindsight, the reporting accountant will normally have the benefit of consultation with the auditors of the individual accounts and of access to their working papers.

Context responsibilities

4.24 *The Stock Exchange Yellow Book* (Section 3 Chap 2 para 1.8) and CA 1985 s 61 respectively require the written consent of any expert (including reporting accountants) to be given to the issue of listing particulars or a prospectus which includes his statement in the form and context in which it is included. It is not clear in law what responsibility this requirement imports for statements made in the document outside the accountant's report, but irrespective of any legal responsibility or otherwise, as a minimum precaution, reporting accountants should be satisfied that the directors and any other experts have, prima facie, reasonable grounds for making the statements contained therein. Particular attention should be paid to the directors' explanations of the trend of profits to the relationship between the accountant's report on past activities and present status and the directors' view of the company's prospects, to the disclosure in the prospectus of material post-balance sheet events, and to any similar information which might be considered to be influential in investment decisions.

4.25 In practice, the matters the reporting accountant should cover in his work in order to satisfy his responsibilities include, inter alia (references are to *The Stock Exchange Yellow Book* Section 3 Chap 2):
(a) profit forecasts (7.2);
(b) particulars of loan capital and of other borrowings (5.16);
(c) analysis of sales turnover or of gross trading income for the last three years between the more important activities (4.3);
(d) adequacy or otherwise of working capital (2.19);
(e) estimate of net proceeds of the issue and statement as to their application (2.18(i));
(f) aggregate emoluments of directors during the last completed financial period together with an estimate of the amount payable to directors, including proposed directors, for the current financial period under arrangements in force at the date of the prospectus (6.3);
(g) exceptional factors influencing the group's activities in the past three years (4.7);
(h) material investment (either 10% of the investee's capital or representing 10% or more of the company's profits or net assets) (5.13);
(i) directors interests in transactions (6.5)

Accounting and internal control

4.26 An investor responding to an invitation to invest is justified in assuming that the basic accounting systems, which have produced the financial information given by the reporting accountants, will be adequate to meet future demands and that his investment will not be jeopardised by a breakdown in accounting communication. The reporting accountant should therefore, decide whether the company has a satisfactory system of accounting and internal control and whether the directors are adequately and promptly informed by the accounting department of the company's progress. This involves a detailed review of management accounting and reporting practices; serious dissatisfaction on these matters combined with refusal to take remedial action should lead to withdrawal from the engagement. It is therefore essential to the interests of the company and the sponsors of the issue that the reporting accountant's work is directed so as to enable him to form a view of these matters at as early a stage in the investigation as possible.

Qualified or restricted opinions

4.27 Where a report is qualified, the reporting accountant is required to explain all the reasons for the qualification together with a quantification of the effect if this is both relevant and practical (*The Stock Exchange Yellow Book* Section 4 para 8).

4.28 However, a report containing any significant qualification or reservation as to *any* of the profits or losses reported on, or as to the balance sheets, is unlikely to be regarded by the Quotation Department as acceptable to support an application for listing. In this respect, the department's practice is to regard a report as unqualified if at least one party to a joint accountants' report has not expressed any reservation therein. Representation should be made through the company's brokers or by direct approach when desirable.

4.29 In particular, *The Stock Exchange Yellow Book* requires early consultation to take place where a report is being prepared in respect of a Class 1 acquisition and it appears that it may be appropriate to qualify the reporting accountant's opinion in respect, either of the final balance sheet or, of the results of any of the three latest years.

4.30 Whether or not a report would be acceptable to the Quotations Department, the reporting accountant should decline to allow his name to be associated with any document when there is a serious deficiency in information casting doubt on any of the last three years to be covered, in particular when the trend of profits might be materially distorted. A similar deficiency affecting only either or both of the first two years in the case of a report covering five years, would necessitate his disclaimer of opinion on the period in question but would not preclude his participation.

4.31 This policy is also supported by the Institute of Chartered Accountants in England and Wales in its statement 3.916 'Accountants' Reports for Prospectus Purposes and Similar Documents; Absence of Detailed Stock Records' issued in January 1972.

Causes of reservations or withdrawal

4.32 Clearly the seriousness of a deficiency in information leading to considerations of withdrawal or disclaimer will depend on individual circumstances, but all alternative means of confirming the results or financial position should be followed in reaching a decision. The most frequent cause of reservations by reporting accountants is that insufficient evidence had been retained to satisfy them that stocks and work-in-progress were properly and consistently ascertained and valued throughout the period of their report.

4.33 In verifying stocks and work-in-progress, the reporting accountant's work, in addition to tests of the primary records, will generally include:
(a) reviewing system of stock controls and stocktaking procedures applying in the period;
(b) examining stock summaries and supporting records;
(c) reviewing auditors' working papers;
(d) comparing the detailed profit and loss accounts and obtaining satisfactory explanations of unusual variations;
(e) considering key ratios;
(f) ensuring that apparent discrepancies arising during the period have been properly investigated and explained.

Technical requirements 145

4.34 These or other secondary or corroborative tests might of themselves, in the absence of stocktaking records, provide satisfactory evidence that the results for the period concerned and financial position are fairly stated.

Form of reservation

4.35 It is generally the case that the missing information which necessitates disclaimer of the reporting accountant's opinion was available to and was examined by the auditors in carrying out their audit of the accounts of the year, or years in question, and that an unqualified audit opinion was given on those accounts. In such an event, the reporting accountant should seek confirmation from the auditors acting for the periods for which records are no longer available that they examined these records during their audit and should satisfy himself that there are no grounds for believing the results to be unreasonable.

4.36 Forms of restricted opinions are given in Practical Guide **4.7**.

The subject entity

Identification

4.37 Disclosure of names of subsidiaries is required to be made in the general body of the listing particulars or prospectus and their repetition in the accountants' report may be of little use to the reader, especially in the cases of large groups. Similarly, a long recital of changes in the composition of the group during the period covered by the report may confuse, or at least detract from the readability of the report. However, the methods of accounting for major acquisitions and disposals of subsidiaries (including changes in their status from or to associated companies) are fundamental to true and fair presentation and should be defined in the statement of accounting policies.

Companies under common ownership

4.38 Problems often arise for reporting accountants when a group structure is imposed for the purpose of the issue on a number of companies which have previously been under common management and control. The usual procedure in these circumstances is to exchange shares at nominal amounts in proportion to the relative contributions to group equity and these exchanges are accounted for on a merger basis. Thus, unless any valuations of assets are made, historical costs will be retained and a consistent basis of profit measurement maintained. Accounting policies should be established for the group as a whole and applied consistently by each member throughout the reporting period. The composition of the 'marketable package' raises more difficult problems where there has been some element of selectivity from a number of companies under common management and control. Criteria adopted as the basis for selection might be the profitability or otherwise of each company, or its cohesion within a vertical or horizontal trading structure or within a geographical pattern, or some other criterion. Before agreeing to act, the reporting accountant should be satisfied that the package selected is a fair one; the merchant bankers and others concerned with the issue will also be interested in this aspect.

4.39 When selection of companies has taken place by reference to acceptable criteria, the reporting accountants must give careful consideration to the form and content of their report. The disclosure provisions of the Companies Acts relating to directors' interests in contracts (CA 1985 ss 232, 317 and Sch 6 Pt 1) should be applied to companies in which directors or substantial shareholders of the reporting company have had an interest during the five years covered by the report, even though the accountants are satisfied as to the commercial basis of these transactions.

Acquisitions and mergers

4.40 Acquisitions and mergers should be treated in accordance with SSAPs 14, 22 and 23.

Imputed interest

4.41 The amount of the consideration specified in a purchase and sale agreement made at arm's length will not generally reflect the real, or fair, purchase price when a payment of the consideration, or a material part thereof, is deferred under the terms of the agreement and there is no provision for interest or the rate of interest prescribed is a nominal one. Clearly, the present value of a stipulated sum payable at a future time is less than the stated amount payable, and the failure to recognise the interest element in the consideration is similar in effect to ante-dating the acquisition. In these circumstances, therefore, or when the consideration is prepaid, interest should be imputed at an appropriate rate, less tax, and the purchase consideration adjusted accordingly.

4.42 What constitutes an appropriate rate of interest is a matter of judgment. It may be noted that the rate imputed by SSAP 3 in calculating earnings per share in certain circumstances is that yielded by an undated government stock (2½% consols in this case). This rate may be regarded as a useful base rate which may require adjustment depending on the term of the deferral, the risk factors, including the cash position of the borrower, and so on. Caution should be exercised in adjusting a rate of interest that is specified in the agreement; prima facie, the stipulation of a rate implies that the parties to the transaction attempted to evaluate the various factors involved.

4.43 Except as indicated above, notional interest adjustments should not normally be made.

Supplementary financial information

4.44 Occasionally, especially when relatively large acquisitions have been made in the latter part of the period reported on, the company, or its financial advisers, will ask the reporting accountant to disclose pre-acquisition earnings of the acquired undertaking as an indication of group earnings potential. The position is compared with an acquisition taking place after the close of the latest accounting period for which a separate report by accountants is required.

4.45 Before giving information on the pre-acquisition results of acquired

undertakings the reporting accountant should be satisfied on the following matters:
(a) The books and accounts of the acquired undertaking for the pre-acquisition period concerned have been subjected to the same degree of examination as in the case of the parent company and other subsidiaries;
(b) the profits records are segregated in the report so that there is no ambiguity over the profits of the company seeking a listing and those of another company with which it had no financial relationship in the relevant periods;
(c) full disclosure is made of the date and terms of the acquisition; and
(d) the attribution of fáir values on acquisition has not vitiated comparison between pre-acquisition results (based on historical costs) and post-acquisition results (based on fair values, or current costs of assets at the date of acquisition).

Disposals of subsidiaries or businesses

4.46 The sale of a subsidiary or business involves changes in the amount and composition of the net assets of the remaining entity. In order to preserve continuity of the profits and net assets statements, and also because accounts are a record of management, the results of the severed subsidiary, or business, should be taken up in the profits statement up to the point of sale and its net assets included in the summary of balance sheets at the relevant dates. It will normally be appropriate to disclose these results and net assets separately in the respective profits and assets statements with an accompanying explanation of the circumstances so that the results, profitability and net assets of the surviving undertaking can be clearly seen.

4.47 Exclusion from the accountant's report of the results and assets of severed undertakings, even those unrelated to activities now being carried on, should be avoided unless there are very unusual circumstances.

Adjustments to profits and assets

Need for adjustments

4.48 In making their report, reporting accountants are required to make such adjustments (if any) to audited accounts as are in their opinion necessary for the purpose of the prospectus (*The Stock Exchange Yellow Book* Section 4 para 4). As indicated in defining the objectives of the accountant's report, financial statements, whether in the form of audited annual accounts, listing particulars or prospectus reports, are read by investors for their independent confirmation of financial position and results.

Matters requiring adjustment

4.49 Broadly, there are two situations that necessitate adjustments to profits and assets:
(a) where there has been a material change in accounting policies applied during the period covered by the report, or acceptable accounting principles have not been applied; and
(b) when material facts have come to light relating to events or transactions

which occurred in a prior period, the accounting effects of which could not be determined with reasonable assurance because of some major uncertainty then existing.

Changes in accounting policies

4.50 Intelligent deductions from profit and profitability trends may be rendered difficult, or even impossible, if the sequence of results and resources employed is broken by changes in important accounting policies. At best, an additional burden of calculating or estimating the effect of the change is thrust upon the reader. Thus, in order that the record of results and resources may be presented coherently, it is vital that it is based on a consistent application of accounting policies that are presently adopted and are to be applied in the future. Restatement of prior years' results and net assets must be made when changes in accounting policies have taken place.

Hindsight

4.51 Adjustments to the profits of prior periods and to corresponding net assets should not be made in respect of the normal recurrent corrections and adjustments which are the natural consequence of the use of accounting estimates. For example relatively immaterial adjustments to provisions for liabilities (including taxation) made in prior periods should be regarded as recurring items to be reflected in the operations of the current period. Similarly, uncertainties concerning the realisation of assets (eg the collectibility of debts, recovery of deferred costs, or realisability of stocks) would not normally give rise to prior period adjustments because the ultimate fact of realisation is dependent upon economic facts occurring after the balance sheet date. As a general rule, a prior period adjustment will relate to a matter of such uncertainty, at the accounting date, as to require disclosure of the fact, and of the uncertainty, in the relevant accounts, and could have been expected to have led to a qualification in the auditors' report thereon, or to the correction of a material accounting error (ie an error of such significance as to be fundamental to the true and fair view and hence the validity of the accounts concerned).

Exceptional, non-recurring or extraordinary items

4.52 Exceptional, non-recurring or extraordinary items call for explanation rather than exclusion. Reporting accountants should not attempt to forecast the future on behalf of investors but should disclose all relevant information concerning the past. Every business encounters an exceptional, nonrecurring or extraordinary event at some time or other, and an investor is just as capable as the reporting accountant in deciding upon its significance if given the facts.

4.53 The profit and loss account should reflect all profits and losses recognised in the period covered by the account other than the effects of a change in accounting policy or correction of a material error (which give rise to prior year adjustments), or unrealised surpluses on revaluation of fixed assets, which should be credited to reserves. Any movements on reserves during the period covered by our report, other than revaluation surpluses, should therefore, be adjusted in the profit and loss accounts.

Different accounting dates

4.54 CA 1985 s 227 (4) and SSAP 14 require a holding company's directors to secure that, except where in their opinion there are good reasons against it, the financial year of each of its subsidiaries shall coincide with the company's own financial year. Reasons for the accounting dates not being co-terminous are to be disclosed.

4.55 These reasons are of paramount importance in considering whether adjustments should be made in the accountants' report to achieve uniform accounting dates throughout a group. Clearly, if there are sound commercial reasons for different dates and no change in practice is contemplated, reporting accountants must decide whether or not the group accounts give a true and fair view of results and financial position on that basis. If dissatisfied, practical changes must be made and the results and net assets of previous periods adjusted accordingly. When restatement is necessary, interim accounts, prepared if necessary for the purpose of the prospectus, should be used whenever possible in preference to time apportioned accounts. Before resorting to time apportionment it is necessary to ensure that the business cycle is short, regular, and devoid of seasonal influences and that a fair portrayal of trend would result from time apportionment.

Fixed assets stated at valuation

4.56 When fixed assets (eg properties) are valued on the basis of a valuation made during the period or after the last accounting date, it will not be appropriate to adjust prior years' depreciation charges based on cost, or on an earlier valuation, because the latest valuation will relate to the assets as now existing and to current valuation data. Post-valuation depreciation charges, however, will be based on the amount of the valuation, and when the valuation is made for the purpose of the prospectus and is to be taken up in the books, it is essential that a note is made in the accountants' report of the amount of future depreciation charges based on the valuation, for comparison with amounts previously charged in the profits statement. It should also be ensured that the future level of depreciation is reflected in profit forecast.

Subsequent events

4.57 Disclosed adjustments to reflect events occurring after the last balance sheet date, eg taking up the estimated proceeds of the offer or the elimination of interest on bank borrowings which are being repaid by means of the offer, are generally inappropriate, even when the issue has been underwritten. In the first instance, the future receipt of proceeds of the issue is but one of a number of events of material significance occurring within or outside the normal course of business since the accounting date, all of which should be portrayed if the context is to be maintained. The second instance involves hypothesis; the facts are that the business was financed by borrowed money at rates of interest then applicable and will in future be financed by equity or debt funding.

Documents required by The Stock Exchange

4.58 The documents required to be submitted to the Quotations Department of The Stock Exchange by reporting accountants include, in addition to their report:
(a) letters of consent to the issue of the prospectus with the inclusion therein of the accountants' formal report and, where appropriate, the accountants' report on the directors' profit forecast, in the form and context in which they are included. (See Practical Guide **4.8**);
(b) statement of adjustments.

4.59 These documents are also required to be available for inspection, generally at the offices of the solicitors to the issue, for a minimum period of 14 days after publication of the prospectus.

Letters of comfort

4.60 In certain cases, the issuing house may request the reporting accountants to write a private letter confirming information relating to statements which the issuing house and/or the directors are required to make in the prospectus or circular. Specimen letters are set out in Practical Guide **4.8**.

4.61 *The Stock Exchange Yellow Book* Section 3 Chap 2 para 2.19 requires that the directors of the company state that in their opinion the company's working capital is sufficient for the requirements of the business, or if not, how it is proposed to provide the additional working capital thought by the directors to be necessary. It is customary for the directors and the issuing house to ask the reporting accountant to review and report to them on the cash flow forecast prepared for this purpose, and this may include a request for a report on the assumptions on which it is based.

4.62 Generally, the approach to such an assignment involves obtaining and reviewing the forecasts prepared by management of the company concerned and comparing the cash flow shown by these forecasts with the facilities and resources available, or to become available, to the company. The extent of the facilities and resources available should be confirmed directly to the reporting accountant by the appropriate third party.

4.63 The forecasts, which should normally cover at least one year from the date of the relevant document, should include forecasts of profit, cash flow and financial position at the end of the period together with detailed assumptions used in the preparation of such forecasts. The reporting accountant will be required not only to check the arithmetical accuracy of the forecasts and that they are properly derived from the assumptions, but also that the assumptions are reasonable, based on historical experience of the company and management's intentions for the future. The degree of review required will in part depend on management's historical accuracy in forecasting and on the surplus of resources over the estimated cash flow requirements. The statement entitled 'Accountants' Reports on Profit Forecasts' issued in 1978 by the accountancy bodies provides guidance in this area.

Technical requirements 151

4.64 The report should clearly identify the information on which the opinion is based. It should only be issued after the reporting accountant has satisfied himself as to the care with which all the directors have considered that information as they, the directors, have sole responsibility for the statement as to the adequacy of working capital.

4.65 The form of report will normally be that, in the opinion of the reporting accountant;
(a) the directors' statement has been made with due care and the forecast is properly compiled on the footing of underlying assumptions; or
(b) it is reasonable for the directors to make their statement.

4.66 *The Stock Exchange Yellow Book* (Section 3 Chap 2 para 5.16) also requires that there should be shown, in relation to the company and its subsidiaries as at the most recent practicable date (which must be stated):
(a) the total amount of any loan capital outstanding in any member of the group, and loan capital created but unissued, and term loans, distinguishing between loans guaranteed, unguaranteed, secured (whether the security is provided by the issuer or by third parties) and unsecured;
(b) the total amount of all other borrowings and indebtedness in the nature of borrowing of the group, distinguishing between guaranteed, unguaranteed, secured and unsecured borrowings and debts, including bank overdrafts and liabilities under acceptances (other than normal trade bills) or acceptance credits or hire purchase commitments;
(c) all mortgages and charges of the group; and
(d) the total amount of any contingent liabilities or guarantees of the group.
An appropriate negative statement must be given, where relevant, in the absence of any such loan capital, borrowings and indebtedness and contingent liabilities.

4.67 In setting out borrowings, inter-company liabilities within the group should normally be disregarded, a statement to that effect being made where necessary. As regards bank indebtedness, where practicable it is recommended that cash book figures should be shown and that they should be reconciled to bank confirmations to ensure there is no unusual pattern of transactions around the relevant date.

4.68 The date at which borrowings and bank indebtedness are stated will usually be other than the accounting year-end date. Thus the reporting accountant will generally have less evidence on which to support the establishment of the correct figure for borrowings than would be the case at the year end. In these circumstances he will have to place significant reliance on management as to the identification of those parties from whom there are outstanding borrowings. These should be sustained by direct confirmation from the lenders of the amounts outstanding at the relevant date.

Statements of adjustments

4.69 The statement of the adjustments must be submitted in draft form to the Quotations Department at least 14 days prior to the date on which it is proposed to publish the prospectus. A specimen statement of adjustments is set out in Practical Guide **4.9**.

FIELDWORK

Planning

4.70 The reporting accountant's report is required by The Stock Exchange to include an expression of opinion on whether or not a true and fair view of the company's (or group's) results, source and application of funds and state of affairs is given by the financial statements included in the accountant's report. Consequently, the reporting accountant should carry out procedures to obtain relevant and reliable evidence sufficient to enable him to form such an opinion at the time of his report. The detailed procedures carried out for this purpose will differ from those which an auditor would carry out year by year.

4.71 The extent of the work which the reporting accountant will need to carry out in relation to his report may be significantly influenced by two important considerations:
(a) whether all financial statements to be reported upon have previously been subjected to audit; and
(b) whether the reporting accountant himself audited the financial statements on which the report is to be based. (This consideration is dealt with in **4.78** below.)

4.72 Where the auditor also acts as reporting accountant, it is desirable for the partner in charge of the audit work to involve another partner in the prospectus work, so as to provide a fresh view of the matters reported on.

4.73 Where material financial information has not been audited it will usually be necessary to carry out additional work on it, before it can be included in the accountant's report, in order to ensure that it can provide a satisfactory basis for his opinion. The extent of the additional work should be planned in detail and, even if he is not carrying out the detailed work himself, the reporting accountant should be closely involved in its planning.

4.74 Additional work will normally be required, eg where the latest financial period reported on by the company's auditors ended more than six months before the date of the prospectus (or nine months in the case of a transaction on the USM) and thereby The Stock Exchange's normal requirement, regarding the maximum period of time between the date of the figures to be reported upon and the date of the report, will not have been satisfied. In these circumstances, an audit of financial statements drawn up to an interim date will normally be required. Additional work will also be required where financial information has been a constituent part of audited financial statements without having been the specific subject of an audit opinion, eg the results of a single division or branch of a large company.

Evidence

4.75 The reporting accountant, in order to form an opinion as to whether the figures incorporated within his report give a true and fair view, will review and discuss with management the features and trends of the results during the relevant period, thereby enabling him to acquire the detailed understanding necessary for the purposes of providing a meaningful presentation in his report.

4.76 The reporting accountant should also review the audit working papers relating to the period to be covered by his report, and he should pay particular attention to any difficult or contentious points which came to light during the course of the audit and to the manner in which they were settled. In carrying out this review he should seek to assure himself that the audit conclusions reached with regard to the relevant financial statements were supported by adequate audit evidence, that the audit work was in accordance with good practice and, with approved auditing standards. It must be emphasised, however, that the fact that an audit has previously been carried out does not alleviate the burden of responsibility for the opinion given by the reporting accountant.

4.77 In addition, the reporting accountant should undertake a general assessment of the company's accounting systems and records relating to the period to be covered by his report in order to determine their reliability as sources of evidence. This work should pay particular attention to difficult or contentious points which have come to light during the course of his discussions with management and to other matters critical to the ascertainment of profit, and therefore to his report, such as evidence concerning the physical existence and basis of valuation of stocks and work-in-progress.

4.78 The reporting accountant should also seek information from the auditor concerning the latter's examination of important areas, and he should obtain clarification from the auditor of any significant accounting matters which have come to his attention during his discussions with management. In this way, and with the benefit of the hindsight generally available to the reporting accountant, he should assess the extent to which he is able to rely on audit work already performed and determine the further procedures which he considers necessary. The reporting accountant does not generally undertake detailed audit procedures relating to earlier years and if he is unable to obtain the assurance he seeks from his review of audit working papers, he will have to consider whether he is able to obtain the evidence he requires from such records as are available. Where the auditor is the reporting accountant, the work described in **4.75** to **4.77** will be carried out by the other partner involved in the prospectus work. Where the reporting accountant is not the auditor, it will be necessary for him to liaise with the auditor and to be able to make full use of the auditor's working papers.

4.79 If the reporting accountant cannot satisfy himself as to the results in all material respects by the procedures outlined above, and it is impracticable for him to repeat auditing procedures, then his reservations should appear in his report. If he believes his reservations to be fundamental, he should not allow his name to be associated with the prospectus. However, if additional assurance is required by the reporting accountant only in respect of the latest period under review, then it may still be possible to arrange for supplementary audit procedures in the relevant areas to be carried out.

REVIEW OF FINANCIAL STATEMENTS

4.80 The reporting accountant will need to review the relevant financial statements to determine, inter alia, whether any adjustments are required thereto for the purposes of his report. A practical approach may be to carry out this review of financial statements concurrently with a review of the audit working papers. Areas upon which the reporting accountant should concentrate during a review of financial statements will include the following:
(a) consideration of whether relevant material events, which may have taken place subsequent to the time of preparation and audit of the financial statements, require adjustments to ensure that they are accounted for in the correct period;
(b) consideration of whether material expenditure or revenue of a non-recurring nature may have arisen in circumstances which require it to be eliminated from normal operations and disclosed separately as an extraordinary or exceptional item; and
(c) consideration of whether material changes in accounting policies may have been applied during the period covered by the report, and may therefore require adjustments in order to provide valid comparisons between financial statements prepared on a consistent basis.

4.81 In carrying out this review, the reporting accountant will need to give special attention to any matters which have given rise to qualified audit reports. He will also need to consider carefully the significance of any such qualifications on his own report. In the case of a quantified qualification, it may be possible to make adjustments to the reported results to eliminate the need to qualify the accountant's report. However, in the case of a fundamental qualification, giving rise to an adverse opinion or to a disclaimer of opinion, or in the case of an unquantified qualification, there may be instances where it will not be possible to express an opinion that a true and fair view is given.

4.82 The reporting accountant will need to review the appropriateness of all the accounting policies, as well as their compliance with accounting standards and the consistency of their application. It is essential to ascertain that all the financial statements encompassed by the accountant's report are set out on the basis of current accounting policies.

4.83 In respect of current cost financial statements set out within the prospectus, the reporting accountant will have additionally to review the working papers supporting the current cost statements to ensure that they are drawn upon the basis stated and are in accordance with the appropriate accounting standard or statement. The current cost accounts should be adjusted as appropriate for the purpose of the accountant's report.

4.84 Analytical review will assist the reporting accountant in determining whether adjustments need to be made to any of the annual financial statements. Explanations of trends, ratios and other statistics should help to indicate whether or not items have been recorded within the correct accounting period. In particular, 'abnormal' items should be highlighted and dealt with accordingly in the analytical review of trading results. Key areas which will be covered by review procedures will include sales trends and gross and net profit margins, as any material fluctuations need to be adequately explained if the reporting accountant is to obtain confidence for his report.

4.1 Stock Exchange documents: summary of listing and other requirements

Transaction	Documents required	Reporting accountants
(1) A listed company makes an offer for the shares of another listed company.	(a) An offer document will be required. (City Code Rule 10 & 15) (b) In certain circumstances, the offeror may decide to publish a profit forecast.	(a) An offeror will often commission reporting accountants to produce a long-form report (b) If a profit forecast is published, an accountant's report on the forecast must also be commissioned—City Code Rule 16 (c) (If a profit forecast is published, any financial adviser mentioned in the offer document must also report on the forecast—City Code Rule 16 (c).
(2) A listed company makes an offer for the shares of an unlisted company.	(a) No special documents are required to be published—City Code introduction paragraph 7 (b) Between the parties involved, there will be letters of intent etc.	(a) A prospective purchaser will often commission reporting accountants to produce a long-form report.
(3) Class 1 Acquisition or Disposal. ie an acquisition or disposal of an unlisted or listed company or assets where the relative figures amount to 15% or more in respect of any one of the following: (i) the value of the assets acquired or disposed of compared with the assets of the acquiring or disposing company (ii) net profits (before taxation and extraordinary items) attributable to the assets acquired or disposed of compared with those of the acquiring or disposing company (iii) aggregate value of the consideration given or received compared with the assets of the acquiring or disposing company.	– Class 1 Announcement—Yellow Book Section 6 Chap 1 para 3.8. The contents of the announcement are described in paragraph 4.2 of that chapter. – Where a Class 1 transaction takes place for cash, a letter on the working capital of the acquiring or disposing company must be submitted to the Quotations Department—para 3.7 of that chapter. (The contents of such a letter are specified in the Yellow Book Section 2 Chap 1 para 5.15.) – Class 1 Circular—Yellow Book Section 6 Chap 1 para 3.1. (The contents of such a circular in respect of an acquisition are set out in the Yellow Book Section 6 Chap 1 para 3.5. The Quotations Department must be consulted on the contents of a circular in respect of a realisation).	– Generally a Class 1 circular should include an accountants' report on the business being acquired—Yellow Book Section 6 Chap 1 para 3.5. The contents of the report are also specified in that paragraph. This requirement may be relaxed on application to the Stock Exchange to the extent that: (1) adequate information has already been issued to shareholders, (2) the company being acquired is already listed and adequate information is available in the statistical services and other publications—Yellow Book Section 6 Chap 1 para 3.6.

157

Transaction	Documents required	Reporting accountants
(iv) equity capital issued by the company as consideration of an acquisition compared with the equity capital previously in issue – Yellow Book Section 6 Chap 1 para 3.1.	If shares are issued which increase any class of shares in issue by 10% or more, listing particulars are required—Yellow Book Section 3 Chap 1 para 3.1.	– Where an issuing house is required to prepare a letter on working capital, reporting accountants may be commissioned to prepare a report on a profit and working capital forecast and on the adequacy of working capital. – A prospective purchaser will often commission reporting accountants to produce a long-form report.
(4) Class 2 Acquisition or Disposal ie an acquisition or disposal where the relevant figures fall between 5% and 15%—Yellow Book Section 6 Chap 1 para 4.1 (see Class 1 definition above)	– Class 2 Announcement—Yellow Book Section 6 Chap 1 para 4.2. – Acquisition or disposal agreement. If shares are issued which increase any class of shares in issue by 10% or more, listing particulars are required—Yellow Book Section 3 Chap 1 para 3.1.	– There is no formal requirement for the involvement of reporting accountants. – A prospective purchaser will often commission reporting accountants to produce a long-form report.
(5) Class 3 Acquisition or Disposal ie a transaction where any comparison on the bases described in (3) above is less than 5% in Yellow Book Section 6 Chap 1 para 5.1.	– Class 3 Announcement is only required if the consideration is wholly or partly in the form of securities for which a listing is sought—Yellow Book Section 6 Chap 1 para 5.2. If shares are issued which increase class of shares in issue by 10% or more, listing particulars are required—Yellow Book Section 3 Chap 1 para 3.1. – Where the consideration is in the form of cash or non listed securities no announcement is required but may be made if the company wishes to make the information available—Yellow Book Section 6 Chap 1 para 5.2. – Acquisition or disposal agreement.	

Stock Exchange documents

Transaction	Documents required	Reporting accountants
(6) Class 4 Acquisition or Disposal ie in principle, a transaction involving a director or a substantial shareholder for detailed definitions see Yellow Book Section 6 Chap 1 para 6.1. (NB for Class 4 only, 'acquisition or disposal of assets' includes an option to acquire or dispose of assets—Yellow Book Section 6 Chap 1 para 1.2.)	– The Stock Exchange may require that a circular should be issued and that the transaction should be subject to shareholder approval. If a circular is required its contents would be specified by Yellow Book Section 6 Chap 1 para 6.2. If shares are issued which increase class of shares in issue by 10% or more, listing particulars are required—Yellow Book Section 3 Chap 1 para 3.1.	– If a circular is required, the Stock Exchange may require that an accountants' report should be included. – A long-form report may be commissioned.
(7) Very substantial acquisitions or reverse takeovers ie A listed company acquires an unlisted company and the relevant figures are 100% or more—see Class 1 transaction definition above Yellow Book Section 6 Chap 1 paras 2 and 7.	– Listed company's shares are suspended until the transaction is approved by the shareholders. Yellow Book Section 6 Chap 1 para 7. – Listing particulars are required and acquiring company is usually treated as a new applicant for listing—Yellow Book Section 6 Chap 1 para 7.	– An accountant's report is normally required—Yellow Book Section 6 Chap 1 para 7 and Section 3 Chap 1 para 3.1.
(8) A listed company applies for re-listing of its shares after suspension.	– The procedure will depend on the circumstances. In some cases the suspension will be lifted following an announcement. In others the suspension will only be lifted after approval of the proposal in general meeting and publication of listing particulars—Yellow Book Section 1 Chap 1 para 15.	– An accountant's report would be required for listing particulars—Yellow Book Section 3 Chap 1 para 3.1. The contents of the report would be determined by the Yellow Book Section 4.
(9) A listed company issues shares by way of a bonus to existing shareholders.	– A circular together with an allotment letter.	– Reporting accountants are not involved.
(10) A listed company issues shares by way of a rights issue to existing shareholders.	– Listing particulars are required—Yellow Book Section 3 Chap 1 para 3.1. – The company may decide to include a profit forecast.	– There is no requirement for an accountant's report. – If a profit forecast is published, an accountant's report on the profit forecast would be required.
(11) A listed company issues shares privately for cash.	– Listing particulars are required—Yellow Book Section 3 Chap 1 para 3.1. – The company may decide to include a profit forecast.	– There is no requirement for an accountant's report. – If a profit forecast is published, an accountant's report on the profit forecast would be required.

Transaction	Documents required	Reporting accountants
(12) An unlisted company applies for listing of its securities either by (i) a prospectus issue (ii) an offer for sale (iii) a placing, or (iv) an introduction	– Listing particulars are required in each case. The contents vary and are specified in Yellow Book Section 3 Chap 1 para 3.1.	– An accountant's report will be required for inclusion in the listing particulars—Yellow Book Section 3 Chap 2 para 5.1. The report must be made by 'independent accountants'—Yellow Book Section 14 para 2.
(13) An unlisted company makes an offer for the shares of a listed company.	– An offer document will be required. – The company may decide to publish a profit forecast.	– Where a profit forecast is published an accountant's report on the forecast will be required.

4.2 Unlisted securities market: requirements in respect of securities of a company seeking admission to the USM

		Reference to USM 'Green Book' Section C
1	Full name of company	1
2	'Care and responsibility' statement by directors	2
3	Statement that admission to listing is *not* being sought	3
4	Particulars of share capital 　authorised 　issued or to be issued 　amount paid up 　description and nominal value	4 (a)
5	Statement that no material issue within 1 year without approval in general meeting	4 (b)
6	If 10% of voting capital unissued, statement that no issue to be made to alter control for nature of business of company without approval in general meeting	4 (c)
7	On consolidated basis: (a) loan capital (issued and unissued), mortgages and charges, and (b) other borrowings or similar indebtedness (incl overdrafts, acceptances (other than normal trade bills), HP commitments, guarantees etc) *Note* negative statements required if appropriate 　　ignore inter-company liabilities (and state so)	5
8	Name, address and description of directors (plus, if required by SE, former names, nationality or former nationality)	6
9	Name and qualification of secretary	7
10	Situation of registered office (and transfer office, if different)	7

	Reference to USM 'Green Book' Section C

11 Names and addresses of: 8
    bankers
    brokers
    solicitors
    registrars
    trustees (if any)

12 Name, address and qualification of auditors   9

13   10
(a) Date and country of incorporation
(b) Authority under which incorporated
(c) If not incorporated in UK, address of head office and principal place of business (if any) in UK

14 Where application is in respect of shares: 11
(a) voting rights of shareholders
(b) if various classes, rights of each class re
    dividend
    redemption
    creation or issue of shares ranking
    pari passu or in priority to all but lowest class of equity
(c) summary of consents necessary for variation of rights

15 Provisions in articles etc regarding   12
(a) power of director to vote on an item in which he is materially interested
(b) power of directors to vote themselves remuneration
(c) directors' exercise of borrowing powers
(d) retirement/non-retirement of directors under an age limit

16 Where application is in respect of loan capital, rights and security (if any)   13

17 General nature of business   14

18 If two or more material (profit/loss or assets) activities, indication of relative importance   14

19 If group trades outside UK, geographical analysis of operations   14

		Reference to USM 'Green Book' Section C
20	Particulars of subsidiaries/associated companies dealt with in accounts, and other material investments 　name 　date and country of incorporation 　private/public 　general nature of business 　capital issued/held	15 (a)
21	For all group companies/prospective subsidiaries 　　particulars of properties 　　principal products 　　number of employees	15 (b)
22	Three year history of sales/gross trading income by trading activity	16
23	Financial and trading prospects (incl. all potentially material special trade factors/risks not mentioned elsewhere)	17 (a)
24	If profit forecast included, give 　　principal assumptions 　　report by auditors on calculations/bases 　　report by financial advisors on 'due care and enquiry'	17 (b)
25	If fixed income securities, profits cover and net tangible assets cover	17 (c)
26	Statement of waiver of future dividends	17 (d)
27	Adequacy of working capital statement	18
28	If for cash (or for cash in past two years), statement of application of proceeds of issue	19
29	Financial statistics giving profits/losses for past five years and: 　　turnover 　　depreciation/amortisation 　　investment/other income 　　interest payable 　　leasing/hire charges 　　exceptional items 　　share of associated companies' results 　　profits/losses before tax and extraordinary items 　　tax (UK, overseas, associated COB)	20 (a)

	Reference to USM 'Green Book' Section C
minorities preference dividends attributable to equity shareholders pre extraordinaries extraordinary items (and related tax) profit attributable to equity shareholder	
30 Financial statistics–assets/liabilities at past five year ends	20 (b)
31 Rate and amount of dividend by class of share	20 (c)
32 Principal accounting policies (and changes/effects in period)	20 (d)
33 Movements on reserves	20 (e)
34 Any other information re 29 and 30 above	20 (e)
35 Statement that last three years accounts were not qualified, or nature of qualifications (plus explanations of directors, if relevant)	20 (f)
36 Material changes in financial extraordinary position since last published accounts, or negative statement	20 (g)
37 Information as in 29–36 above re acquisitions/agreed acquisitions since last date in financial statistics	21
38 Particulars of non-cash share issues by any group company in past two years, or negative statement	22
39 Particulars of cash share issues by any group company in past two years, or negative statement	23
40 Particulars of options (or agreements to grant options) over capital of any group company, or negative statement	24
41 Preliminary expenses, and by whom payable	25 (a)
42 Expenses of issue and flotation (if not 41 above) and by when payable	25 (b)
43 Discounts, commissions, brokerages etc on issue/sale of any capital or any group company in past two years, or negative statements	26

		Reference to USM 'Green Book' Section C
44	Alterations in share capital of company in past two years	27 (a)
45	Directors' interests (split beneficial/non-beneficial) in company's shares or negative statement	27 (b)
46	Other substantial interests (ie not directors') in company's shares or negative statement	27 (c)
47	Directors' existing/proposed service contracts (not determinable by company without compensation within one year), or negative statement	28 (a)
48	Aggregate directors' emoluments in last financial year, and estimate for current financial year (incl proposed directors)	28 (b)
49	Full particulars of directors' interests in promotion of or in property transactions with any group company, or negative statement	29 (a)
50	Full particulars of director's material interests in contracts or arrangements with any group company, or negative statement	29 (b)
51	Outstanding claims or litigation, or negative statement	30
52	Name of any promoter	31 (a)
53	Any cash, securities or other benefits to promoter in past two years, or proposed, and consideration therefor	
54	Experts' consents to publication ('form and context')	32
55	Tax clearances, or indemnities	33 and 34
56	Material contracts outside normal course of business in past two years	35

57	Inspection of documents (place and time)
	    memorandum and articles
	    directors' service contracts
	    material contracts (58 above)
	    experts' reports/statements
	    experts' consents
	    audited accounts for last three financial years
		36

4.3 Companies Act requirements for prospectuses

(NB—Not applicable to applications for listing of securities on Stock Exchange—See Practical Guide **4.4**)

Matters to be specified in a prospectus (contd)	*Reference to CA 1985 Sch 3*
1 Particulars of the number of founders, management or deferred shares and the nature and extent of any interests of the holders in the profits and property of the company.	para 1 (a)
2 Directors' share qualifications if fixed by the Articles.	para 1 (b)
3 Any provision in the Articles as to directors' remuneration.	para 1 (b)
4 Names, descriptions and addresses of the directors.	para 1 (c)
5 Minimum subscription where shares are offered to the public and details of whether to be utilised in whole or part to provide for the following:	para 2
(a) purchase of property in whole or part from the issue;	para 2
(b) preliminary expenses and commission for subscribing or procuring subscriptions for shares or debentures;	para 2
(c) repayment of monies borrowed in respect of working capital; and	para 2
(d) amounts required for items 5(a) and (b) other than out of the issue.	para 2
Shares may not be allotted where minimum subscription is not achieved.	
6 Date of opening and duration of subscription lists.	para 3
7 Amounts payable on application and allotment of each share including share premium.	para 3
8 For each offer in the previous two years, the amounts offered for subscription, actually allotted and paid on allotment including share premium.	para 5
9 Particulars of shares and debentures in the company under an option stating: (a) price; (b) duration of option; (c) consideration for which option granted;	para 4

Matters to be specified in a prospectus (contd)   *Reference to CA 1985 Sch 3*

(d)   name of grantee (where options are granted to all members or class of members or employees state this without giving names of grantees).

10   Numbers of shares or debentures issued other than for cash in the previous two years and if partly paid, the extent of the payment.   para 5

11   Amounts payable, paid in respect of:
(a)   commission (other than to sub-underwriters) on subscription or procuring subscription for shares and debentures in previous two years. Show rate of commission;   para 10
(b)   estimated preliminary expenses;   para 10
(c)   estimated expenses of the issue;   para 10
(d)   benefit paid or given to any promotor of the issue in the previous two years and consideration for the benefit/payment.   para 10

12   Dates, nature and parties to contracts entered into in the previous two years which were not in the ordinary course of the business.   para 11

13   Names and addresses of auditors.   para 12

14   Particulars of interests of any director in the promotion of or acquisition of property by the company in the previous two years. If the director is a partner in a firm involved in such a transaction, detail the extent of the director's interests in that firm. Also include a statement of amounts received in cash, shares or otherwise for services rendered or as an inducement to become a director.   para 13

15   Where the prospectus offers shares for public subscription, detail all classes of shares and their rights with respect to voting, capital and dividends.   para 14

16   The prospectus must be dated and, if in respect of any shares or debentures of a company incorporated outside Great Britain, it must contain details of: CA 1985 s 63
(a)   date and place of incorporation;   CA 1985 s 72
(b)   instrument defining/constituting incorporation and the Acts/provisions effecting that incorporation;
(c)   registered office;
(d)   if principal office is in the UK give the address.

17   If the business has been carried on less than three years since acquisition/formation this should be stated.   para 15

Matters to be specified in a prospectus (contd)	*Reference to CA 1985 Sch 3*
18 The prospectus must be signed by all directors and proposed directors and lodged with the Registrar of Companies together with necessary consents from any professional experts and copies of contracts detailed in paragraph 13 of Schedule 3 before it may be published.	CA 1985 ss 64 and 65
19 In respect of property acquired/to be acquired in whole or in part out of proceeds of issue (unless in ordinary course of business or immaterial): (a) vendors' names and addresses; (b) amount payable to each vendor; (c) short particulars of any transaction relating to property within past two years in which vendor/promoter/director had any interest.	para 7

Reports to be made	*Reference to CA 1985 Sch 3*
1 Auditors must report on: (a) profits or losses of the company or group for the 5 preceding financial periods;	para 16
(b) rate of dividend and amount absorbed thereby for each class of share for each of the 5 preceding financial periods;	para 16
(c) details of any waiver of dividends;	para 16
(d) balance sheet or consolidated balance sheet at end of last financial period.	
2 If report is in respect of a period ending earlier than three months before publication, a statement that no accounts have been made up since that date.	para 16
3 Where a company acquires a subsidiary after the last date to which accounts have been made up and audited, a report by a named qualified accountant with respect to: (a) profits or losses of the acquired business (and any subsidiary companies) attributable to interest acquired in respect of each of the previous five completed financial periods; (b) the assets and liabilities of the business on the balance sheet of the company; (c) any other relevant matters.	paras 16 and 17

4.4 Contents of listing particulars (new listing)

1 The following is a highly abbreviated summary of the information required to be included in listing particulars for a new listing of shares. It should therefore be used with caution, and reference should be made to *The Stock Exchange Yellow Book* in any cases of doubt.

2 It mainly follows the order of Section 3 Chap 2 of *The Stock Exchange Yellow Book*. The information in listing particulars need not follow that order precisely, provided always that it is set out in a form that can be analysed and understood as easily as possible.

The issuer, the persons responsible for listing particulars, the auditors and other advisers	*Reference to Section 3 Chap 2 of The Stock Exchange Yellow Book*
1 Name, registered office (head office, if different)	1.1
2 Date, country of incorporation, and length of life (if limited)	1.2/1.3
3 Legislation under which issuer operates, and legal form adopted thereunder	1.4
4 Place of registration and registered number	1.5
5 Names, addresses and functions of persons responsible for listing particulars	1.6
6 Declaration by persons responsible for listing particulars (usually directors)—see *The Stock Exchange Yellow Book* for text	1.7
7 Experts' consents ('form and context')	1.8
8 Names, addresses and qualifications of auditors for past three years	1.9

9 Names and addresses of
    bankers
    brokers
    solicitors
    solicitors to issue
	1.10

172 *Contents of listing particulars (new listing)*

The securities for which application is being made	*Reference to Section 3 Chap 2 of The Stock Exchange Yellow Book*
10 Statement that 'Application (has been) (will be) made to the Council of The Stock Exchange for (the securities) to be admitted to the Official List'	2.1 (a)
11 Securities available to public?	2.1 (b)

12 Other stock exchanges where
    admission to listing being sought
    same class of securities already listed
	
	2.2
	2.3

13 Indication of other markets (not listings) on which securities of same class are dealt	2.4
14 Resolutions etc whereby securities created and/or issued	2.5
15 Nature and amount of issue	2.6
16 If predetermined, number of securities (to be) created and/or issued	2.7

17 Particulars of shares for which listing sought
    number
    nominal value per share
    designation or class
    coupons attached
	2.8

18 Summary of rights of shares being listed
    voting
    participation
    special rights
	2.9

19 Time limit after which dividend entitlement lapses and to whom	2.10
20 Provisions re changes in capital and variation of class rights	2.11

21 Tax on income withheld at source
    in country of origin
    in UK
	2.12

22 Issuer assumes responsibility for withholding of tax at source?	2.13

Contents of listing particulars (new listing)

	Reference to Section 3 Chap 2 of The Stock Exchange Yellow Book
23 Arrangements for/restrictions over transferability of securities	2.14
24 Fixed dates (if any) on which divided entitlement arises	2.15
25 Names and addresses of 　　registrars 　　paying agents in UK	2.16
26 Securities registered or bearer?	2.17
27 If separate issue or marketing (whether public or private) is being made, or has been made within previous 12 months, of the securities for which admission is sought, additional detailed information is required—see *The Stock Exchange Yellow Book*	2.18
28 Directors' adequacy of working capital statement	2.19
29 Payment/benefit to promoter (if required by general law)	2.20
30 If shares being placed, and none previously sold to public 　　number of shares 　　nominal value 　　minimum offer price (where applicable)	2.21 (a)
31 Dates of admission to listing/commencement of dealing (if known)	2.21 (b)
32 Indication of any public take-overs of or by the issuer in current and previous financial years, and price/terms and outcome of such offers	2.21 (c)
33 If, in conjunction with the issue, shares of any class subscribed for privately, give details	2.22
34 If securities for which listing sought offered by way of rights or capitalisaton issue, give additional information—see *The Stock Exchange Yellow Book*	2.23

174 Contents of listing particulars (new listing)

General information about the issuer and its capital | *Reference to Section 3 Chap 2 of The Stock Exchange Yellow Book*

35 Principal objects, and reference to source — 3.1

36 Particulars of share capital (by class of share) — 3.2
    authorised and issued
    agreed to be issued
    still unpaid

37 If issuer has authorised but unissued capital, or commitment to increase capital, indication of — 3.3
    amount and, where appropriate, duration of authorisation
    categories of persons with preferential subscription rights re such capital
    terms and arrangements for the share issue corresponding to such additional portions of capital

38 Number/main characteristics of non-capital shares (if any) — 3.4

39 If 10% or more of voting capital unissued, statement that no material issue to be made within one year of issue — 3.5

40 Amount and conversion terms of any outstanding convertible debt securities — 3.6

41 Changes in issued share capital in past three years (give price, terms etc), or negative statement — 3.7

42 Indication of persons who may, jointly/severally and directly/indirectly, control issuer, and proportion of voting capital held — 3.8

43 Name of any person (not director) interested, and amount of interest, in 5% or more of issuer's capital, or negative statement — 3.9

44 If issuer a member of a group — 3.10
    brief description of group
    issuer's position therein
    if a subsidiary, names and interests of holding companies

45 Investment in own shares, if not disclosed separately in balance sheet — 3.11

	Reference to Section 3 Chap 2 of The Stock Exchange Yellow Book
46 Particulars of options granted (or agreed to be), or negative statement	3.12
47 Tax clearances and indemnities	3.13 and 3.14
48 Material legal/arbitration proceedings against group in previous 12 months, or negative statement	3.15
49 Material contracts outside normal course of business within past two years	3.16
50 Period (min 14 days) and place documents available for inspection 　　memorandum and articles 　　trust deed 　　material contracts (49 above) 　　directors' service contracts (85 below) 　　if takeover/merger etc, relevant documents 　　experts' reports, statements and consents 　　statement of adjustments 　　audited accounts for past two financial years	3.17
51 Statement re definitive documents of title if bearer securities—see *The Stock Exchange Yellow Book*	3.18

The group's activities

52 Principal activities and products/services sold/performed	4.1
53 Significant new products/activities	4.2
54 Analysis of turnover for past three years 　　by category of activity 　　by geographical market (where categories or markets differ substantially)	4.3
55 Relative importance of material (in profit, asset or other terms) activities	4.4
56 Particulars of principal establishments (ie ones accounting for more than 10% of turnover or production)	4.5
57 Principal place of business (if any) in UK	4.6

176 *Contents of listing particulars (new listing)*

	Reference to Section 3 Chap 2 of The Stock Exchange Yellow Book
58 Exceptional factors affecting 52 to 57 above	4.7
59 Summary of dependence on patents, contracts etc, where of fundamental importance	4.8
60 Research and development policy over past three years, where significant	4.9
61 Significant business interruptions in past 12 months	4.10
62 Average numbers employed (and changes, if material) over past three years, if possible by activity	4.11
63 Main investments (quantified) in other undertakings over past three years and in current year	4.12
64 Other principal investments being made, geographical spread, and method of financing	4.13
65 If listing particulars prepared re merger/takeover etc aggregate value of consideration how satisfied full particulars of variation (if any) in total directors' emoluments of issuer, or negative statement	4.14
66 Principal future investments (if any) (except firm commitments re other undertakings)	4.15

Financial information concerning issuer or group

67 Accountants' report covering last five completed financial years and dealing with profits/losses, assets/liabilities, financial record and position of group Notes – see separate checklist on contents of accountants' reports (Practical Guide **4.5**) – variation if any member of group was a listed company in last 12 months—see *The Stock Exchange Yellow Book* – if group, must be consolidated information – if group, parent company information may be omitted (with SE consent) if does not provide significant additional information	5.1

5.5
5.5 |
| 68   Annual accounts audited? Give details of refusals or qualification of audit opinions | 5.3 |

	Reference to Section 3 Chap 2 of The Stock Exchange Yellow Book
69 Any other information in listing particulars audited?	5.4
70 EPS and dividend per share for past three years (adjusted where necessary for share issues)	5.6 and 5.7
71 Waiver of future dividends?	5.8
72 If more than nine months since last published annual accounts, include interim financial statement covering at least first six months (state if unaudited)	5.9
73 Significant changes in financial or trading position last end of last period included above, or negative statement	5.10
74 If accounts do not give true and fair view, additional information may be required	5.11
75 Source and application of funds for past three years	5.12
76 Information regarding investments in related/ associated companies and subsidiaries (a) name and address of registered office (b) activity (c) proportion of capital held (d) issued capital (e) reserves (f) profit/loss on ordinary activities after tax (g) carrying value in issuer's own balance sheet (h) amounts unpaid on shares held (i) dividends received in last financial year (j) debts owed by/to issuer *Note* (e) and (f) may be omitted if related company or subsidiary does not publish annual account (e), (f), (g) and (i) may be omitted if related company or subsidiary consolidated/equity accounted for by issuer	5.13
77 Name, registered office and proportion of capital held for each investment of more than 10% of capital not covered in 76 above, unless immaterial	5.14
78 Disclose consolidation principles if not UK GAAP	5.15 (a)
79 List (or indicate in list under 76 above) companies which are material to assessment of issuer	5.15 (b)

178 *Contents of listing particulars (new listing)*

	Reference to Section 3 Chap 2 of The Stock Exchange Yellow Book

80   Details of borrowings (consolidated) at latest practicable date:
(a)   loan capital (issued/unissued, secured/unsecured)
(b)   other borrowings etc (guaranteed/unguaranteed, secured/unsecured)
(c)   mortgages and charges
(d)   total contingent liabilities/guarantees
or negative statement re (a), (b) or (d)   5.16

The management

81   Names, addresses, functions, business interests and activities of
      directors
      unlimited partners (if limited partnership with share capital)
      founders, if issuer less than five years old   6.1

82   Name/qualification of secretary   6.2

83   Aggregate directors' remuneration in last financial year, and estimate for current year (incl proposed directors)   6.3 (a) and (c)

84   Waivers of dividends by directors   6.3 (b)

85   Directors' existing/proposed service contracts (not determinable by issuer without compensation within one year), or negative statement   6.4

86   Full particulars of directors' interests in unusual/significant transactions, or negative statement   6.5

87   Directors' interests (split beneficial/non-beneficial) in shares of group companies, or negative statement   6.6

88   Loans/guarantees by group to directors   6.7

89   Staff share schemes in group   6.8

90   Provisions in articles etc regarding   6.9
      power of director to vote on an item in which he is materially interested
      power of directors to vote themselves remuneration
      directors' exercise of borrowing powers
      retirement/non-retirement of directors under an age limit

Contents of listing particulars (new listing) 179

The recent development and prospects of the group

Reference to Section 3 Chap 2 of The Stock Exchange Yellow Book

91   General information on trend of business since last financial year/published accounts, and particularly most significant recent trends in production, sales, stocks; state of order book; trends in costs/selling prices

7.1 (a)

92   Prospects for current year (incl all potentially material special trade/other factors/risks not mentioned elsewhere)

7.1 (b)

93   If profit forecast included, give
    principal assumptions
    report by accountants on calculations/bases
    report by financial advisers on 'due care and
      enquiry'

7.2

4.5 Checklist—contents of an accountant's report (listed companies)

	Reference to Section 4 of The Stock Exchange Yellow Book	Tick or N/A
1 Name of accountants giving report	3	
2 Date of report	3	
3 If report is in respect of period ending earlier than three months before publication, a statement that no accounts made up since that date.	3	
4 At least the following for each of the five completed financial years prior to publication (or since incorporation/commencement of business if later):		
(a) Net turnover (as per CA 1985) Cost of sales (where appropriate, show distribution and administration expenses separately) Investment and other income Interest payable Exceptional items Share of results of related companies Profit/loss before tax and extraordinary items Tax (UK, overseas and related companies—indicating basis) Minority interests Preference dividends Profit/loss attributable to equity shareholders before extraordinaries Extraordinary items (showing attributable taxation) Profit/loss attributable to equity shareholders *Dividends, by class of share (give rates and any waivers) Any other relevant items Increase/decrease in retained profits for the year	3 (a)	

---

*Not required in respect of Class 1 acquisition either of a company which is *not* a listed company, or of assets whether representing a business or otherwise.

Checklist—contents of an accountant's report (listed companies)

		Reference to Section 4 of The Stock Exchange Yellow Book	Tick or N/A

	Also, by way of note, give
	  amortisation, deprecation and obsolescence of fixed assets
	  leasing and hire charges
	  directors' remuneration
	  auditors' remuneration
		3 (a)
		(ii)	

*(b)	Post tax profit/loss and divided, both per share	3 (b)	
(c)	Movements on reserves not shown in profit and loss account	3 (c)	
(d)	Balance sheets or, where appropriate, the assets/liabilities of the business In the case of a group the consolidated balance sheet must be given, and also the parent company if it shows significant additional information	3 (d)	
(e)	Source and application of funds statement	3 (e)	
*(f)	Any interest capitalised (give also indication of amount and treatment of any tax relief)	3 (g)	
(g)	The principal accounting policies	3 (h)	

*5 As at the end of the last period, a statement as regards   3 (f)
(a) bank loans/overdrafts
(b) other borrowings
analysed between the aggregate amounts repayable
  under one year
  one to two years
  two to five years
  over five years

6 Any other matters which appear to be relevant for the purposes of the report   3 (i)

7 Reports must normally   5
(a) comply with SSAPs, and
(b) pay attention to SORPs
Significant departures from SSAPs must be disclosed and effects quantified
NB   (a)   The relevant standards are those applicable to the last financial year reported on.

---

*Not required in respect of Class 1 acquisition either of a company which is *not* a listed company, or of assets whether representing a business or otherwise.

Checklist—contents of an accountant's report (listed companies)

	Reference to Section 4 of The Stock Exchange Yellow Book	*Tick or N/A*

(b) Wherever possible appropriate adjustments should be made to show profits for all periods in accordance with these standards

8 All appropriate adjustments for purposes of report must be made by reporting accountants, and   4
(a) report must contain statement that all/no adjustments were made;
(b) a separate Statement of Adjustments reconciling figures in report with published figures must be prepared
(NB – Statement of Adjustments must be signed by accountants and made available for public inspection
– must be submitted to Quotations Dept for approval at least 14 days before publication of report)

9 If material proportion of profit arises or assets situated overseas, give indication of their amount/source or situation   9

10 Give names, addresses and professional qualifications of any valuers, accountants or other experts whose opinions or reports are referred to in the report   13

11 Additional statutory disclosures in annual report resulting from company's business must also be made in an accountant's report   12

12 Accountants must report in accordance with current practice (ie Auditing Standards, guidelines etc)   3

13 True and fair view opinion to be given   7

14 If reservation about material matters, must qualify. Reasons for (and where relevant/practical quantification of effect of) qualification must be given   8

Foreign Companies

	Reference to Section 4 of The Stock Exchange Yellow Book	Tick or N/A
15 Reports re foreign companies must comply with all the above (but subject to the following). A report will not normally be acceptable unless audited in accordance with or up to UK standards	10	
16 Report may be acceptable covering a shorter period than normal (see details in *The Stock Exchange Yellow Book*)	11	
17 Reports should comply with International Accounting Standards applicable at end of last period reported on (other than IAS14—segmental reporting)	5	

4.6 Specimen accountant's report

The Directors,   (Accountant's name)
Allington Enterprises plc,
W G Grantley Ltd (Merchant bankers)   (date)

Gentlemen,

We have examined the audited accounts of Allington Enterprises plc (the company) and its subsidiary companies (the group) for the five years ended 31 December 1982. We have acted as auditors throughout the period.

The financial information set out below under the heading 'Historical Cost Accounts' is based on the audited accounts of the group after making such adjustments as we considered appropriate.

In our opinion, based on our examination and the reports of certain associated companies not audited by us, the consolidated profit and loss accounts, balance sheets and statements of sources and application of funds together with the notes thereon set out in Part 1 below, give a true and fair view of the profits and source and application of funds of the group for each of the periods stated and of the state of affairs of the group at the dates stated.

No accounts have been prepared for submission to members since those for the year ended 31 December 1982.

The financial information set out in Part II below under the heading 'Current Cost Accounts' is also based on the audited accounts after making such adjustments as we considered appropriate. In our opinion, the current cost statements have been properly prepared in accordance with the policies and methods set out in the notes thereto and with the notes give the information required by Statement of Standard Accounting Practice No 16.

PART 1 HISTORICAL ACCOUNTS

Allington Enterprises plc and its subsidiary companies

Accounting policies

The significant accounting policies adopted in preparing the financial information set out below are as follows:

1 *Accounting convention*
The accounts are drawn up on the historical cost basis or modified by the revaluation of certain fixed assets.

2 *Basis of consolidation*
The group accounts are based on a consolidation of the audited accounts of the company and its subsidiaries made up to 31 December in each year.

3 Goodwill
It is the company's policy to attribute fair values to the net tangible assets on the acquisition of a subsidiary or associated company. The goodwill represents the amount by which the purchase consideration on acquisition exceeds these fair values.

4 Foreign currencies
Assets and liabilities in foreign currencies are translated into sterling at the closing rate of exchange at each accounting date. Exchange differences arising are taken to profit and loss account.

5 Turnover
Turnover represents the charges to customers outside the group, excluding value added tax and sales taxes, for goods supplied or work carried out.

6 Engineering and construction contracts
Profit earned under contracts is accounted for on a proportion of completion basis in the case of contracts occupying more than a year's work, and otherwise on completion. Provision is made for all losses under these contracts immediately they are known or can be foreseen.

7 Stocks and work in progress
Stocks and work in progress (other than under long term contracts) are stated at the lower of cost (including as appropriate all production and site overheads) and estimated net realisable value.

Work in progress under long term contracts is stated at cost plus attributable profit, less foreseeable losses and after deducting progress billings.

8 Contract maintenance and guarantees
Provision is made for the cost of maintenance and remedial work which may be necessary under guaranteed performance contracts.

9 Research and development
Expenditure on research and development is charged against revenue as incurred.

10 Depreciation
Depreciation is provided by the straight line method on the cost or valuation, less residual value, of all fixed assets, other than freehold land, based on their estimated useful lives. The rates of depreciation in respect of fixed assets other than freehold buildings vary from 10% to 25%.

11 Deferred taxation
Deferred taxation is provided at current rates of taxation in respect of timing differences only where it is expected that a taxation liability or recovery will arise in the foreseeable future.

ALLINGTON ENTERPRISES plc AND ITS SUBSIDIARY COMPANIES

Consolidated Profit and Loss Account

Years ended 31 December

	Notes	1978 £000	1979 £000	1980 £000	1981 £000	1982 £000
TURNOVER	1,2	8,147	9,597	10,502	12,971	17,607
TRADING PROFIT	1,2	896	1,027	1,092	1,336	1,849
Share of profits of associated companies	3	63	89	96	162	149
Investment income	4	38	42	35	57	61
		997	1,158	1,223	1,555	2,059
Interest payable on loan capital	5	15	15	15	15	175
PROFIT BEFORE TAXATION AND EXTRAORDINARY ITEMS		982	1,143	1,208	1,540	1,884
Taxation	6	442	525	511	637	742
Profit before extraordinary items		560	618	697	903	1,142
Extraordinary gains and (losses)	7	–	80	60	–	(104)
PROFIT AFTER TAXATION AND EXTRAORDINARY ITEMS		560	698	757	903	1,038
Dividends	8	100	100	100	200	200
RETAINED PROFITS		460	598	657	703	838
Earnings per share based on ordinary shares in issue						
Before extraordinary items		11.2p	12.3p	13.9p	18.1p	22.8p
After extraordinary items			14.0p	15.1p		20.8p
Dividends per share		2p	2p	2p	2p	2p
STATEMENT OF RETAINED PROFITS						
Retained profit brought forward		191	651	1,209	1,906	2,609
Profits retained for the financial period		460	598	657	703	838
Retained profit carried forward		651	1,249	1,906	2,609	3,447

ALLINGTON ENTERPRISES plc AND ITS SUBSIDIARY COMPANIES

Consolidated Balance Sheets

Years ended 31 December

	Notes	1978 £000	1978 £000	1979 £000	1979 £000	1980 £000	1980 £000	1981 £000	1981 £000	1982 £000	1982 £000
FIXED ASSETS											
Intangible assets—goodwill			718		718		718		718		718
Tangible assets	9		4,838		4,967		5,364		6,053		8,784
Investments	10		663		716		813		1,186		1,372
			6,219		6,401		6,895		7,957		10,874
CURRENT ASSETS											
Stocks and work in progress	11	2,163		2,425		2,812		3,101		3,675	
Debtors		1,408		1,595		1,699		2,114		2,419	
Cash at bank and in hand		62		83		77		995		374	
		3,633		4,103		4,588		6,210		6,468	
CREDITORS (amount falling due within one year)											
Bank overdrafts		661		561		537		62		141	
Creditors		1,775		1,814		2,065		2,275		2,912	
Taxation		670		746		805		938		1,201	
Dividends payable		88		88		88		150		150	
		3,194		3,209		3,495		3,425		4,404	
NET CURRENT ASSETS			439		894		1,093		2,785		2,064
TOTAL ASSETS LESS CURRENT LIABILITIES			6,658		7,295		7,988		10,742		12,938
CREDITORS (amounts falling due after one year)											
8% Debenture stock 1996–2001 (secured)	12	–		–		–		2,000		2,000	
6% Mortgage loan		250		250		250		250		250	
			250		250		250		2,250		2,250
PROVISIONS FOR LIABILITIES AND CHARGES											
Deferred taxation		757		796		832		883		1,053	
Deferred capital grants		–		–		–		–		100	
			757		796		832		883		1,153
			5,651		6,249		6,906		7,609		9,535
CAPITAL AND RESERVES											
Called up share capital			5,000		5,000		5,000		5,000		5,000
Revaluation reserve			–		–		–		–		1,088
Profit and loss account			651		1,249		1,906		2,609		3,447

ALLINGTON ENTERPRISES plc AND ITS SUBSIDIARY COMPANIES

Statements of Source and Application of Funds

Years ended 31 December

	1978		1979		1980		1981		1982	
	£000	£000	£000	£000	£000	£000	£000	£000	£000	£000
SOURCES OF FUNDS										
1 *Profit before taxation and extraordinary items*		982		1,143		1,208		1,540		1,884
Items not involving the movement of funds:										
2 Depreciation	615		669		680		842		1,174	
3 Surplus on sale of fixed assets	(32)		(62)		–		(56)		(49)	
4 Profit retained by associate companies	(33)		(50)		(51)		(92)		(79)	
		550		557		629		694		1,046
Funds generated by operations		1,532		1,700		1,837		2,234		2,930
Other sources										
5 Proceeds of sale of fixed assets	103		166		60		390		80	
6 Issue of 8% debenture stock 1996–2001	–		–		–		2,000		–	
7 Government capital grants	–		–		–		–		100	
		103		166		60		2,390		180
		1,635		1,866		1,897		4,624		3,110
APPLICATIONS OF FUNDS										
8 Purchase of fixed assets	(1,042)		(822)		(1,077)		(1,865)		(2,848)	
9 Purchase of investments	(45)		(3)		(46)		(281)		(107)	
10 Taxes paid	(206)		(410)		(416)		(453)		(309)	
11 Dividends paid	(100)		(100)		(100)		(138)		(200)	
		(1,393)		(1,335)		(1,639)		(2,737)		(3,464)
		242		531		258		1,887		(354)
Changes in working capital										
12 Debtors	(107)		(187)		(104)		(415)		(305)	
13 Creditors	170		39		251		210		533	
14 Stocks	(165)		(262)		(387)		(289)		(574)	
		(102)		(410)		(240)		(494)		(346)
Change in net liquid funds		140		121		18		1,393		(700)

ALLINGTON ENTERPRISES plc AND ITS SUBSIDIARY COMPANIES

Notes to the Accounts

1 DETAILED TRADING ACCOUNT

	1978		1979		1980		1981		1982	
	£000	£000	£000	£000	£000	£000	£000	£000	£000	£000
Turnover		8,147		9,597		10,502		12,971		17,607
Cost of sales		5,098		6,742		6,619		8,184		11,064
Gross profit or loss		3,049		2,855		3,883		4,787		6,543
Distribution costs	728		630		946		1,169		1,581	
Administrative expenses	1,457		1,260		1,890		2,338		3,162	
		2,185		1,890		2,836		3,507		4,743
		864		965		1,047		1,280		1,800
Other operating income		32		62		45		56		49
Trading profit		896		1,027		1,092		1,336		1,849

2 TURNOVER AND TRADING PROFIT

An analysis by industrial sectors is set out below:

	Years ended 31 December				
	1978	1979	1980	1981	1982
	£000	£000	£000	£000	£000
(a) *Turnover*					
Steel construction and builders' supplies	2,684	3,097	3,308	4,531	6,486
Engineering	3,197	3,235	3,637	3,830	4,437
Haulage	741	989	1,025	1,176	1,710
Distribution	1,525	2,276	2,532	3,434	4,974
	8,147	9,597	10,502	12,971	17,607
(b) *Trading profit*					
Steel construction and builders' supplies	342	372	377	517	734
Engineering	252	245	267	269	324
Haulage	73	86	94	102	154
Distribution	229	324	354	448	637
	896	1,027	1,092	1,336	1,849

Trading profit is stated after charging/(crediting) the following items:

Depreciation	615	669	680	842	1,174
Hire of plant and machinery	197	215	207	161	106
Interest on bank loans and overdrafts	89	91	104	110	28
Directors' emoluments	–	–	68	106	116
Profits on disposal of plant	(32)	(62)	–	(56)	(49)
Research and development expenses	163	186	211	264	257
Auditors remuneration	16	18	19	22	25

3 ASSOCIATED COMPANIES

Share of net aggregate profits before tax	63	89	96	162	149
Taxation attributable thereto (included in group taxation):					
Corporation tax	13	16	19	30	31
Less: Relief for overseas taxes	10	11	12	22	21
	3	5	7	8	10
Overseas taxes	25	32	33	63	55
	28	37	40	71	65
Share of net aggregate of profits after tax	35	52	56	91	84

4 INVESTMENT INCOME

Listed investments	30	33	31	46	49
Unlisted investments	8	9	4	11	12
	38	42	35	57	61

5 INTEREST PAYABLE ON LOAN CAPITAL

8% Debenture stock 1996–2001	–	–	–	–	160
Mortgage loan repayable after 5 years	15	15	15	15	15
	15	15	15	15	175

	Years ended 31 December				
	1978	1979	1980	1981	1982

6 TAXATION
The charge is based on the profits of each period and comprises:

	1978	1979	1980	1981	1982
Corporation tax	385	483	454	575	670
Less: Relief for overseas taxes	31	47	41	61	69
	354	436	413	514	601
Overseas taxes	68	89	98	123	141
	422	525	511	637	742
Tax deferred (included above)	46	39	36	51	170

7 EXTRAORDINARY GAINS AND LOSSES

	1978	1979	1980	1981	1982
Profit on sale of surplus freehold land	–	80	60	–	(104)
Loss on closure of an overseas branch	–	–	–	–	(104)
	–	80	60	–	(104)

8 DIVIDENDS
Ordinary shares of £1 each

	1978	1979	1980	1981	1982
	100	100	100	200	200
Rates of dividend based on 5,000,000 ordinary shares in issue	2%	2%	2%	4%	4%

9 FIXED ASSETS—TANGIBLE ASSETS
At 31 December 1982:

	Cost or valuation £000	Cumulative depreciation £000	Net book value £000
Freehold land and buildings	2,300	–	2,300
Leasehold property	450	–	450
Plant, equipment and vehicles	11,680	5,646	6,034
	14,430	5,646	8,784

The freehold land and buildings and leasehold property were valued at £2,300,000 and £450,000 respectively by Proudie & Co, Chartered Surveyors, on an existing use basis at 31 December 1982 and are stated at the amount of that valuation. Otherwise all fixed assets are stated at cost, including costs attributed thereto on acquisition of subsidiaries. The estimated useful lives of fixed assets for the purpose of depreciation are set out below:

Freehold land	infinite
Freehold property	50 years
Leasehold property	(tenure of lease expiring in 1999)
Plant and manufacturing equipment	7–15 years
Vehicles	3–5 years
Warehouse and office equipment	10 years

Capital commitments at 31 December 1982

	Group £000
Contracts placed for future capital expenditure	750
Expenditure sanctioned but not yet contracted	500
	1,250

10 FIXED ASSETS—INVESTMENTS

Subsidiary companies:	
Shares at cost, less amounts written off	470
Advances and other indebtedness	402
	113
	985

Associated companies:
Listed investments
Unlisted investments
Loans

Investments in associated companies are stated at cost, less premiums on acquiring shares (included in goodwill), together with the Group's share of retained post-acquisition profits, less losses.

Trade and other long-term investments:	
Listed investments, at cost amount written off	325
Unlisted investments	62
	387
	1,372

Investments in associated companies are represented by aggregate net assets as follows:

	Group £000
Fixed assets (at cost, less depreciation)	
Freehold property (Cost: Group £750,000; Company, £400,000)	500
Plant, equipment and vehicles (Cost: group £1,415,000; Company £492,000)	725
	1,225
Net current assets	503
	1,728
Long term loans	650
Deferred tax	93
	985

Valuations

	Group £000
Associated companies:	
Market values—UK listed companies	414
Directors' valuation of unlisted investments	360
	744
Trade and other long term investments:	
Market values—UK listed companies	285
—Foreign listed companies	75
	360
Directors' valuation of unlisted investments	62
	422

11 STOCK AND WORK IN PROGRESS

Merchandise and finished products		1,083
Partly finished production		798
Contract work in progress		1,802
		3,683
Less:		
Progress billings		651
		3,032
Materials and components		643
		3,675

12 LOAN CAPITAL
The mortgage loan at 6% is repayable by five equal annual instalments beginning 31 December 1990.

13 CONTINGENT LIABILITIES AT 31 DECEMBER 1982
(a) Bills discounted—Group £446,000
                —Company £360,000
(b) Guarantees—Bank overdrafts of overseas subsidiaries, £300,000
            —Bank overdrafts of associated companies—Group £220,000
                                              —Company £100,000

CURRENT COST ACCOUNTS

There should be appended
(a) a current cost balance sheet at 31 December 1982;
(b) Current cost profit and loss account for 1981 and 1982;
(c) notes to the current cost accounts.

Yours faithfully,
(Accountants' name)

4.7 Variations to the specimen accountant's report

1 *The subject entity*
Where there have been significant changes in the nature of the subject entity during the period covered by the accountant's report, it will be necessary to explain these changes in the opening paragraphs of the report. The precise wording naturally depends upon the circumstances. The following, however, are examples of what may be required.

Example 1
XY Limited (the Company) was incorporated on xx January 19xx under the name of X Limited and by the issue of shares immediately acquired from Mr X and members of his family the whole of the issued share capitals of certain companies. At the same date, the Company acquired the assets and assumed the liabilities of and succeeded to businesses hitherto carried on by other companies which were then placed in voluntary liquidation. All these companies had traded under common management and control prior to the acquisition by the Company of their shares or businesses, and their results and assets and liabilities are included in the consolidated profit and loss accounts and balance sheets and are reflected in the statement of source and application of funds set out below throughout the period covered by this report.

Example 2
On 3 January 1980, X Limited changed its name to Y Limited.

2 *Accounts*
Where the last statutory accounts were prepared as at a date more than six months before the prospectus, the Quotations Department will normally require later accounts to be prepared and audited. If this is done, the accountants' report should include the following references:

Example 3
No accounts have been prepared for submission to members since those for the year ended xxx 19xx. Interim accounts for the six months ended xxx 19xxx have been prepared and have been audited for the purposes of this report.

In exceptional cases, the Quotations Department may not require that such further audited accounts should be prepared and audited but may permit the inclusion in the accountant's report of information based on unaudited management accounts. In such cases the 'true and fair' opinion should be restricted so that it applies only to earlier periods and the accountant's report should include an opinion similar to the following:

Example 4
No audited accounts have been prepared in respect of any period since xxx 19xx. However, we have reviewed the management accounts of the companies for the xxx months to xxx 19xx and estimates for the remaining four weeks to xxx 19xx. These accounts have been prepared in accordance with the accounting policies normally adopted by the company after making certain adjustments and on the assumptions that (i) there will be no changes in the present management and business policies of the company which would have an effect on the results when the final accounts covering the year are prepared and (ii) there will be no changes which would alter the accounting policies adopted in drawing up the profit estimates. On the basis of this review, which did not constitute an audit, we report that in our opinion the statement set out below of the unaudited estimated profit and loss account for the year ended xxx 19xx and the unaudited balance sheet at that date have been properly prepared from the management accounts and subsequent estimates.

3 *Reservations*
Where there are reservations to express in the opinion concerning audits in which the reporting accountants were not involved the following example might be appropriate:

Example 5
Stock and work-in-progress records at xxx 19xx and 19xx of certain subsidiary and predecessor companies of the Company have not been retained. Consequently, we have been unable to satisfy ourselves as to the amounts of these assets at those dates and as to the amount and allocation of profits and sources of application of funds for the two years ended xxx 19xx. The auditors confirm that these records were examined by them during the course of their audits and that they are satisfied that the stock and work-in-progress were properly ascertained on consistent bases throughout the period of this report. With this reservation, in our opinion the consolidated profit and loss accounts, balance sheets and statement of source and application of funds give a true and fair view of the profits and sources and application of funds of the Group for the five years ended xxx 19xx and of the state of affairs of the Company and of the Group at the dates stated below.

4.8 Listing particulars and Stock Exchange circulars: accountants' letters

Chapter 3 sets out examples of certain letters to be written in connection with the inclusion of circulars of a report by investigating accountants on a profit forecast and a letter of comfort to be written to an issuing house to support their opinion that a company's working capital is sufficient to meet its requirements.

Consent letter

When the investigating accountant has signed an accountant's report the letter permitting the inclusion of that report in listing particulars, a prospectus or a circular should be in the following form:

> The Directors
> .... (Merchant Bankers)
>
> Gentlemen
>
> We hereby consent to the inclusion of our report dated .... 19 .. on the consolidated profits and sources and applications of funds of ... Limited and its subsidiary companies for the five years ended .... 19 .., the balance sheets of the Group and of the Company at .... 19 .. in the listing particulars dated .... 19 .. in the form and content in which it is included. A final proof of the listing particulars initialled by us for the purpose of identification is attached.
>
> Yours faithfully

Where the report is included in a prospectus, CA 1985 ss 67 and 68 provide that the reporting accountant's responsibilities in relation to his report continue after the issue of the prospectus until the time of allotment. If, before the allotment, the reporting accountant becomes aware of information, which would have led him to believe that a statement which he has made in the report is untrue, s 68(1)(b) would require him to withdraw his consent in writing and give reasonable notice of that fact. Although ss 67 and 68 do not apply in the case of listing particulars, best practice would require a similar course of action to be followed in such a case.

Indebtedness

The issuing house is required to include in listing particulars inter alia a statement with respect to the long term debt and other bank indebtedness of the company at the final balance sheet date. To support this statement, the issuing house may request the reporting accountant to provide a letter of comfort on this point. In such a case, the following form should be used:

The Directors
.... (Merchant Bankers)

Gentlemen

We confirm that the information relating to the indebtedness of the Group at .... 19.. shown in item ... of the Appendix to the document/listing particulars, is fairly stated, so far as concerns debentures on the basis of amounts confirmed by the registrars/relevant trustees, and so far as concerns other indebtedness on the basis of amounts confirmed by the lenders. A final proof of the Appendix initialled by us for the purpose of identification is attached.

Yours faithfully

In setting out borrowings, inter company liabilities within the group should normally be disregarded, a statement to that effect being made if necessary.

As regards bank indebtedness, where practicable, the document should show cash book figures which have been reconciled to bank confirmations to ensure that there is no evidence of an unusual pattern of transactions at around the relevant date. This date will normally be different from the accounting year end date and the reporting accountant will usually have less evidence on which to report than would be the case at the year end. In these circumstances, the reporting accountant is obliged to place considerable reliance on management to identify parties from whom there are outstanding borrowings. These amounts should be substantiated by direct confirmation from the lenders of the amounts outstanding at the relevant date.

Where appropriate, the reporting accountant should refer to the fact that he has placed reliance on the company's records. A suitable wording might be:

'... on the basis of amounts recorded in the records of the Group which amounts agree or reconcile with those confirmed by the lenders.'

Other letters

Issuing houses may request letters on other financial matters. In many cases, such letters can be written on the basis of the examples given above (eg confirmation of information given in listing particulars about contingent liabilities).

Often listing particulars will include a pro forma balance sheet together with a statement of the basis on which it has been prepared (eg where a major acquisition has taken place a pro forma balance sheet will set out a combination of the assets and liabilities of the new and enlarged group). In such cases, the reporting accountant will normally be expected to review the pro forma blance sheet and report to the issuing house that the directors of the company have properly prepared it in accordance with the basis stated.

4.9 Listing particulars and Stock Exchange circulars: specimen statement of adjustments

ALLINGTON ENTERPRISES plc

Statement of Adjustments to Profit and Loss for the five years ended 31 December 1982

	1978 £000	1979 £000	1980 £000	1981 £000	1982 £000	Five year totals £000
PROFITS BEFORE TAXATION AND EXTRAORDINARY ITEMS *As stated in the audited accounts*	981	1,242	1,196	1,543	1,911	
Adjustments						
1 Unfunded pension liabilities—allocation to appropriate periods of unfunded liability met in 1980	(30)	(34)	143			
2 Increase in stocks less additional depreciation of fixed assets on changes in bases of accounting at 1 January 1980	19	21	(85)			
3 Adjustments to contract work in progress on adoption at 31 December 1982 of proportion of completion basis of taking profit on long term contracts	12	(6)	14			
		(80)	(60)			
4 Profit on sale of freehold land treated as an extraordinary item				(3)	(27)	
As stated in the accountants' report	982	1,143	1,208	1,540	1,884	6,757

continued overleaf

201

	1978 £000	1979 £000	1980 £000	1981 £000	1982 £000	Five year totals £000
TAXATION						
As stated in the audited accounts	426	530	546	638	751	
Adjustments						
1 Relief attributable to pension provision	(12)	(15)	63	—	—	
2 Stocks, work-in-progress and depreciation adjustments	8	10	(98)	(1)	(9)	
As stated in the accountants' report	422	525	511	637	742	2,837
PROFIT AFTER TAXATION (as stated in the accountants' report)	560	618	697	903	1,142	3,920
EXTRAORDINARY ITEMS						
As stated in the audited accounts			60		(104)	
Adjustments						
1 Re-designation of income (above)	—	80	—	—	—	
As stated in the accountants' report	—	80	60	—	(104)	36
PROFIT AFTER TAXATION AND EXTRAORDINARY ITEMS	560	698	757	903	1,038	3,956
DIVIDENDS	100	100	100	200	200	700
RETAINED PROFITS						
As stated in the accountants' report	460	598	657	703	838	3,256

Statement of adjustments to the Balance Sheets for the five years ended 31 December 1982

	1978 £000	1979 £000	1980 £000	1981 £000	1982 £000
NET ASSETS					
As stated in audited accounts	5,646	6,263	6,799	7,611	9,553
Adjustments					
1 Unfunded pension provision—reallocation	(18)	(19)	80	—	—
2 Stocks, work in progress and depreciation adjustments	23	5	27	(2)	(18)
As stated in the accountants' report	5,651	6,249	6,906	7,609	9,535

Chapter 5

Bank Presentations

INTRODUCTION	5.01
TECHNICAL BACKGROUND	5.04
FIELDWORK	5.07
CONTENT OF PRESENTATION	5.08
ORGANISATION	5.09
THE BUSINESS OR PROJECT	5.11
MARKETING	5.14
FINANCIAL INFORMATION	5.15
WRITING THE PRESENTATION	5.17
PRACTICAL GUIDES	
Specimen index for bank presentations	5.1
Specimen introduction for bank presentations	5.2

INTRODUCTION

5.01 The other chapters in this Manual have concerned situations in which an independent accountant has been reporting on a particular situation or proposal. In each case, the purpose of the reporting accountant has been to establish what are the facts of a particular case or the foreseeable consequences of a certain proposed course of action. The purpose of this reporting exercise is to enable the principals concerned to decide what course of action should be adopted and to do this on the basis of fact rather than ignorance.

5.02 Circumstances may arise in which independent accountants are asked to act in a related but somewhat different capacity. Companies wishing to raise new funds or to secure the continuance of existing facilities may need to make presentations to banks or to other sources of capital with the purpose of explaining the company's case and the grounds for the provision of finance. Faced with this necessity, the company may find that it lacks staff who have either the skill or experience necessary to prepare a comprehensive and persuasive presentation. Many such companies would look to independent accountants to provide assistance in the preparation of such presentations.

5.03 The purpose of this chapter is to describe the approach which should be adopted to the preparation of such presentations on behalf of a client.

TECHNICAL BACKGROUND

5.04 As is often the case with investigations, there is no available specification of the technical content for bank presentations prepared by independent accountants on behalf of their clients. The nature and content of the presentation are determined on the one hand by the client's desire to present the most persuasive case possible, and on the other hand, by the prospective investor's need for sufficient information to enable a decision to be made. The value of the independent accountant's service to the client lies partly with the accountant's ability to prepare an appropriate solution to these two requirements.

5.05 It may also lie partly in the accountant's ability to suggest to which sources of finance the company might apply for help and how the application might best be structured to maximise the prospects for success. The nature of the advice which is to be given in this way is not dealt with in this chapter.

5.06 There is a danger that through involvement in the preparation of such a presentation and, indeed, in its final submission to the prospective investor, the independent accountant may find that he is regarded as having accepted a greater responsibility for the information which is presented than is justified by the work which has been undertaken. It is important, therefore, that this matter should be resolved at the outset. The independent accountant should discuss with the client the nature of the presentation which is to be made to a prospective investor and explain the costs which may be involved if the reporting accountant is to take full responsibility for the financial information prepared by or on behalf of the client. It should also be made clear how the eventual presentation will be modified to reflect any restriction in the work performed and how the bank may view such restrictions. The approach which is eventually agreed should be recorded in a letter of engagement together with any matters affecting the engagement which have been discussed with the client.

FIELDWORK

5.07 Once the letter of engagement has been agreed, the independent accountant can arrange for the completion of any fieldwork which is necessary. The extent of this work will depend upon the nature of the project which is the subject of the presentation and the degree of responsibility which the independent accountant is to accept for the information included in the presentation.

CONTENT OF PRESENTATION

5.08 In general terms, the subject areas covered by a bank presentation bear some similarity to the subject areas covered by a long-form report discussed in Chapter 2. The difference lies in the depth in which they are described. A specimen index for a bank presentation is set out in Practical Guide 5.1. Each of the principal headings in the specimen index is discussed further below.

ORGANISATION

5.09 One of the first questions which a prospective investor is likely to ask about a venture seeking finance is 'who is involved in this undertaking?'. The experience, imagination, flair and integrity of the team of people principally concerned in an enterprise are of great moment to the investor since the quality of a management team may well be the factor which ultimately determines the success of the business.

5.10 In view of this, the presentation should incorporate a short introductory note on the background of the organisation and of the people who are principally involved in it. This introduction should be frank, acknowledging any weaknesses which are known to exist and the company's plans to correct such weaknesses. If the enterprise is large enough to have a managerial and reporting structure, this also should be outlined in the presentation.

THE BUSINESS OR PROJECT

5.11 Having described the team of people who are involved in the business and its development, the presentation should next completely yet concisely describe the products or services which the business provides or which it intends to provide in the future and for which finance is required. The description should include both the features of the products and the benefits to customers of their use. If the purpose of seeking additional finance is to enable research and development work to be completed, this should be explained together with a description of the project which is being undertaken. The plan for research and development should be described together with the goals and objectives which have been set for the project.

5.12 Technical risks may be involved in undertaking research and development and the presentation should include some reference to these so that the prospective investor has an opportunity to assess them.

5.13 If research and development work has been completed and the product is now being produced or is about to be produced, the presentation should explain the amount of space which is needed, the capital equipment which is involved and the extent of any arrangements with other organisations for the production of goods for sale.

MARKETING

5.14 Prospective investors are likely to be particularly interested in the arrangements which have been made for marketing and selling a new product: any presentation should, therefore, give a clear indication of the market which the enterprise perceives to exist for its products, the arrangements which the business has made to ensure that its products or services are both sold and distributed to that market and, finally, the reasons for the business's expectations. It is easy for a business to become so concerned with the development of a product or service that it forgets the need to sell and distribute the results of its labours. Any prospective investor will need to be convinced that the company making the presentation has avoided this pitfall.

FINANCIAL INFORMATION

5.15 The amount of financial information included in the presentation will depend largely on the state of the company's financial support and the amount of money which the company is seeking. It is important that there should be a clear description of the extent and nature of the financial support which is sought together with a description of the uses to which it will be put.

5.16 If the business has been operating for some time it will also be necessary to describe the financial condition of the business and its recent history. The company should also present financial projections, including sales projections, information on manufacturing, selling and administrative costs, and a cash flow projection. These projections should be accompanied by projections of the complete profit and loss account and balance sheets for a period of time which is appropriate both to the nature of the financial support which is being sought and the quality of the financial information which the company is able to produce. Where projections are required for an extended period and the information is slightly uncertain in nature, consideration should be given to providing guidance on the sensitivity of the projections to fluctuations in the assumptions on which the projections are based.

WRITING THE PRESENTATION

5.17 If an independent accountant becomes involved in the writing of the presentation on behalf of a client, it is important to remember that the presentation is to be made with a purpose of persuading a prospective investor to provide support. This may require a somewhat different type of style and drafting to that normally employed in formal reports by investigating accountants. Wherever possible, professional jargon and prolixity should be avoided in the interest of conveying the client's message to the investor as simply and effectively as possibly. To this end, it is usually valuable to commence the presentation with a summary that enables the reader to gain very quickly a picture of the organisation which is being presented and the nature of its requests. More detailed information can follow. This structure is reflected in the specimen index set out in Practical Guide 5.1.

5.18 One other matter needs to be considered, however. In many cases, the presentation once compiled will be submitted to the prospective investor using the client's own stationery. In such cases, there need be no reference to the involvement of an independent accountant in the preparation of the presentation.

5.19 In other cases, however, the company may wish the presentation to be made using the independent accountant's stationery or, alternatively, the client may wish to refer to the independent accountant in the presentation made on his own stationery. In either case, the independent accountant should ensure that the presentation refers appropriately to any limitations upon the work which the accountant has performed and the responsibility which the accountant can assume for the information which is included in the presentation. Examples of introductory paragraphs which may be useful in this context are set out in Practical Guide 5.2.

5.1 Specimen index for bank presentations

Introduction

Summary
   Nature of the business
   Growth potential of business or project
   Funding required
   Purpose of funding
   Reasons for anticipating success of project

Organisation
   Background to development of business
   Management team
   Strength and weaknesses in team

Business or project
   Description of present and future products
   Advantage of products
   Manufacturing arrangements
   Research and development activities
   Technical risks attaching to research and development
   Patent, trademark, copyright
   Independent evaluation of product or services

Marketing and sales
   Describe expected market
   Describe market segments and geographical location
   Describe size of market and growth
   Describe how sales to market are to be achieved
   Anticipated market share
   Reasons for anticipating market share
   Describe competitors: then strengths and weaknesses

Financial information
   Description of funding request and purpose (combination of debt, equity, etc)
   Anticipated future needs for additional capital
   Pro forma financial data
   Pro forma cash flow projections
   Pro forma profit and loss account projections
   Pro forma projected balance sheets
   Assumptions employed in preparing projections

5.2 Specimen introduction for bank presentations

xxx Bank plc

Gentlemen

Example Company Limited

At the request of our client, Example Company Limited, we have pleasure in enclosing information about the business, its background, financial condition and prospects in support of that company's application for additional/ extended financial support (amend as necessary).

The terms of the application and the justification for it are summarised in Section I: Summary and further details are supplied in succeeding sections.

We have compiled this information from documents supplied by the company and have not performed an audit. The projections which are enclosed have also been compiled by the company, and although we have ensured that they are arithmetically reliable, we have not attempted to review and validate the assumptions and judgments on which they are based.

Index

Accountant
  accounting and internal control, 143
  causes of reservations or withdrawal, 144–145
  contents of report, 140–141, 181–184
  context responsibilities, 142–143
  direct responsibility, 141–142
  form of reservation, 145
  letters,
    consent, 199
    indebtedness, 199–200
    other, 200
  opinion, 142
  qualified or restricted opinions, 143–144
  report for prospectus,
    contents, 140–141, 181–184
    specimen, 185–196
    variations to specimen, 197–198
  reporting,
    responsibility for profit forecast, 76–77
    who is not company's auditor, 142

Accounting dates
  different, 149

Acquisitions
  treatment in prospectus, 146

Adjustments to profits and assets. *See* LISTING PARTICULARS

Aide-memoires
  investigation. *See* INVESTIGATION AIDE-MEMOIRES
  management,
    efficiency, and, 43–59
    financial, 55–59
    personal, 53–55
    production, 48–52
    marketing, 52–53
  profit and working capital forecast review, 103–107

Aims
  aide-memoire, 43–44

Assets
  adjustments to. *See* LISTING PARTICULARS
  fixed, stated at valuation, 149

Associates
  overseas, liaison with, 6

Auditor
  subject company, 8

Balance sheet
  forecasting, 123–124
  summary, investigation aide-memoire, 31–32

Bank
  balance, investigation aide-memoire, 36

Bank—*cont.*
  presentations,
    business or project, 206–207
    content, 206
    fieldwork, 206
    financial information, 207–208
    generally, 205
    marketing, 207
    organisation, 206
    specimen index, 209
    specimen introduction, 211
    technical background, 205–206
    writing, 208

Business
  bank presentation, 206–207
  disposal, 147
  general description, investigation aide-memoire, 18
  nature of, long form report, 63–65

Capital
  employed, long form report, 68–69
  profit and working capital forecast review. *See* PROFIT FORECAST

Cash balance
  investigation aide-memoire, 36

Cash flow
  forecast, 121–123

Circulars. *See* LISTING PARTICULARS

City Code on take-overs and mergers
  profit forecast,
    assumptions on which based, 97–100
    generally, 95–96
    requirements, 78–80

Company
  accounting policies normally adopted by company, 84
  common ownership, under, 145–146
  economic and commercial environment in which operating, 6
  listing particulars. *See* LISTING PARTICULARS
  seeking admission to USM, 161–165
  subject,
    auditors, 8
    information on, 7–8

Cost accounts
  current, 196
  historical, 185–195

Creditors
  provisions and guarantees, investigation aide-memoire, 37–38

Debentures
  investigation aide-memoire, 40

213

214   Index

Debtors
  investigation aide-memoire, 35
Director
  profit forecast, 75–76, 113–114
Documentation. See WORKING PAPERS

Efficiency
  aide-memoire, 43–59
Employees
  investigation aide-memoire, 25–26
Environment
  commercial and economic, consideration of, 6

Fieldwork
  bank presentations, 206
  getting the facts, 7–9
  listing particulars, 152–154
  planning, 4, 7–9
  profit forecast, 88–91
  specific profit and working capital forecast work, 9
  verification work, 9
Financial advisers
  profit forecast, 77–78
  published reports, 91–92
Financial management
  aide-memoire, 55–59
Financial results
  past, investigation aide-memoire, 27–28
Financial statement
  review of, 154–155
  tabulating, 5–6
Future prospects
  long form report, 69

Gross margins
  forecast, 120

History
  investigation aide-memoire, 16
  long form report, 63

Information sources
  auditors, 8
  establishment of other sources, 8–9
  planning, 6–7
  subject company, 7–8
Information systems
  aide-memoire, 47–48
Investigation
  aide-memoires. See INVESTIGATION AIDE-MEMOIRES
  approach to, 3
  detailed guidance, 12
  documentation, 11–12
  fieldwork, 4, 7–9
  organisation. See ORGANISATION
  phases, 3–4
  preparation, 3
  reporting, 4, 9–11

Investigation aide-memoires
  balance sheets summary, 31–32
  bank and cash balances, 36
  creditors provisions and guarantees, 37–38
  debentures, long-term mortgages and loans, 40
  debtors, 35
  general description of business, 18
  generally, 14, 15
  history, 16
  management accounting arrangements, 41
  management and other employees, 25–26
  manufacturing, 20–21
  ownership, 17
  past financial results, 27–28
  premises and plant, 23–24
  prepayments, 35
  purchasing, 19
  selling, 22
  stocks, 33–34
  taxation, 39
  trading results, 29–30
  work in progress, 33–34

Leadership
  aide-memoire, 45–46
Legal matters
  long form report, 57
Letter
  accountant's. See ACCOUNTANT
  consent, of, submission to Stock Exchange, 150–151
  engagement, of, profit and working capital forecast review, 101–102
Listing particulars
  accountant's letter,
    consent, 199
    indebtedness, 199–200
    other, 200
  accountant's report,
    contents, 140–141, 181–184
    current cost accounts, 196
    historical cost accounts, 185–195
    specimen, 185–196
    variations to specimen, 197–198
  accountants' responsibilities and scope of examination, 141–145
  acquisition reports, 141
  adjustments to profits and assets,
    changes in accounting policies, 148
    different accounting dates, 149
    exceptional, non-recurring or extraordinary items, 148
    fixed assets stated at valuation, 149
    hindsight, 148
    matters requiring, 147–148
    need for, 147
    specimen statement, 201–202
    subsequent events, 149
  Companies Act requirements, 167–169
  contents, 171–179

Index

Listing particulars—*cont.*
documents required by Stock Exchange, 150–152
fieldwork,
  evidence, 153–154
  planning, 152
financial statements, review of, 154–155
generally, 139
letters of consent, 150–151
matters to be specified, 167–169
reports to be made, 169
six months rule, 141
statements of adjustments, 151–152, 201–202
statutory requirements, 140
Stock Exchange requirements, 140
subject entity,
  acquisitions and mergers, 146
  companies under common ownership, 145–146
  disposals of subsidiaries or businesses, 147
  identification, 145
  imputed interest, 146
  supplementary financial information, 146–147
  summary of, 157–160
technical requirements, 139–152
unlisted securities market, 161–165

Loan
long-term, investigation aide-memoire, 40

Long form reports
illustration of contents, 61–69
information contained in, 14
investigation aide-memoires. *See* INVESTIGATION AIDE-MEMOIRES
meaning, 14
unpublished, illustration of contents, 115–118

Management
accounting arrangements, investigation aide-memoire, 41
aide-memoire, 43–59
financial, 55–59
investigation aide-memoire, 25–26
personal, 53–55
production, 48–52

Manufacturing
investigation aide-memoire, 20–21

Marketing
aide-memoire, 52–53
bank presentation, 207

Mergers
treatment in prospectus, 146

Morale
aide-memoire, 45–46

Mortgage
long-term, investigation aide-memoire, 40

Net assets
long form report, 68–68

New listing. *See* LISTING PARTICULARS

Organisation
aide-memoire, 45
bank presentations, 206
planning. *See* PLANNING
preliminary review, 4
profit forecast, 85–88
written instructions, 4–5

Overheads
forecast, 120–121

Overseas associates
liaison with, 6

Ownership
investigation aide-memoire, 17
long form report, 63

Personal management
aide memoire, 53–55

Planning
fieldwork, 4, 7–9
plan emphasis, 6
profit forecast, 87–88
reporting 4, 9–11
steps, 5–7

Plant
investigation aide-memoire, 23–24

Policies
accounting,
  changes in, 148
  normally adopted by company, 84
aide-memoire, 44

Preliminary review
form, 4
nature, 4
purpose, 4

Premises
investigation aide-memoire, 23–24

Prepayments
investigation aide-memoire, 35

Presentations. *See* BANK

Production costs
forecast, 120

Production management
aide-memoire, 48–52

Profits
adjustments to. *See* PROSPECTUS
forecast. *See* PROFIT FORECAST
motivation, aide-memoire, 44–45

Profit forecast
accounting policies normally adopted by company, 84
assumptions on which based,
  City Code on take-overs and mergers, 97–100
  detailed considerations, 98–99
  examples, 100
  general rules, 99–100
  requirement to state, 97–98
assumptions used in preparing, 83
balance sheet forecasting, 123–124
cash flow forecast, 121–133

Profit forecast—*cont.*
City Code. *See* CITY CODE ON TAKE-OVER AND MERGERS
computer modelling, 125
directors' responsibility, 75–76, 113–114
documentation, 91
features of, 81–85
fieldwork,
    detailed examination of forecasts, 90
    generally, 88
    results achieved to date, 90
    review of method of preparation, 88–89
    testing reliability of forecasts, 89–90
    working capital forecasts, 90–91
financial advisers' responsibility, 77–78
follow up, 84–85
generally, 73
meaning, 73–74
organisation,
    obtaining detailed written instruction, 87
    planning, 87–88
    preliminary review, 85–87
overhead forecast, 120–121
period covered by, 82
production cost and gross margin forecast, 120
profit and working capital forecast review, aide-memoire, 103–107
    forecasting working papers, 119–135
    specimen letter of engagement, 101–102
    specimen short-form reports, 113–114
    specimen working papers, 109–112
    unpublished long-form report, 115–118
profit figures, latest unaudited, 83–84
publication, 74–75
published, form of, 82–83
reporting,
    consent to extended use of forecasts, 93
    consent to publish, 92–93
    published financial advisers' reports, 91–92
    published short-form reports, 91
    unpublished long-form reports, 93
reporting accountants' responsibility, 76–77
review of calculations, 9
sales forecast, 119–120
Stock Exchange, requirements of, 80–81
technical requirements, 73–85
Prospectus. *See* LISTING PARTICULARS
Purchasing
investigation aide-memoire, 19

Reporting
interpretation and evaluation, 9–10
long form reports. *See* LONG FORM REPORTS
planning, 4, 9–11
profit forecast, 91–93
report,
    editing, 10
    form and content, 10
    presentation, 10
    reading of draft, 11

Reporting—*cont.*
report—*cont.*
    review before printing, 11
    writing, 11
Results
financial, 27–28
trading, 29–30, 53–54

Sales
forecast, 119–120
Securities
company seeking admission to USM, 161–165
Selling
investigation aide-memoire, 22
Short-form reports
meaning, 14
profit and working capital forecast review, 113–114
Specialists
liaison with, 6
Statements of adjustments
submission to Stock Exchange, 151–152, 201–202
Stock Exchange
circulars. *See* LISTING PARTICULARS
documents,
    required by, 150–152
    summary of listing, 157–160
letters of consent, 150–151
profit forecasts, 80–81
prospectus. *See* LISTING PARTICULARS
statements of adjustments, 151–152, 201–202
Stocks
investigation aide-memoire, 33–34
Strategic planning
aide-memoire, 46–47
Subject entity. *See* PROSPECTUS
Subsidiary
disposal, 147

Taxation
investigation aide-memoire, 39
long form report, 69
Trading results
investigation aide-memoire, 29–30
long form report, 65–66

Unlisted securities market
securities of company seeking admission to USM, 161–165

Valuation
fixed assets stated at, 149
Verification work
amount of, 9
review of auditor's working papers, 9

Work in progress
investigation aide-memoire, 33–34

Working capital
   forecast, 106–107
   profit forecast, 90–91
Working papers
   contents, 11–12
   forecasting, 119–135
   format, 11
   object of preparing, 11

Working papers—*cont.*
   profit and working capital forecast review, 109–112
Written instructions
   absence of, 5
   drafting, 5
   obtaining, 4–5